Job◆portunity:

Your Career GPS

Going

Places

Successfully

In the World of Work

Angel M. Swindell Nix, MA, BCC

 Publisher's contact information: The National Institute of Leadership & Organizational Development, LLC, 8611 Concord Mills Boulevard, #201, Concord, North Carolina 28027. www.whatsleadership.com , www.scholarathletics.net & info@whatsleadership.com

ISBN 978-0-9897326-0-4

Attention corporations, universities, colleges, and professional organizations: Quality discounts are available on bulk purchases of this book for educational, gift purposes, or as premiums for increasing magazine subscriptions or renewals. Special books or book excerpts can also be created to fit specific needs. For more information, please contact The National Institute of Leadership & Organizational Development, LLC, 8611 Concord Mills Boulevard, #201, Concord, North Carolina 28027. www.whatsleadership.com & info@whatsleadership.com

Dedication

This book is dedicated to every child who watches or has watched their parents come home from work in a tired, frustrated, angry, and passionless state of being. My hope is that this book will reverse their parents' state of mind concerning work to thereby strengthen and support a happy, healthy home life for the entire family, extended family and hosts of friends impacted by the work life of their loved ones.

Contents

Preface - 10

The universal human need, the response to that need, and YOUR call to action.

Part I: Playing the People Game

Chapter One - 14
Perfecting Your People Skills

Chapter Two - 25
WorkPlace Bullying

Chapter Three - 37
Creating Career Building Relationships

Chapter Four - 44
Developing True Self Awareness

Chapter Five - 55
Achieving Emotional Synergy with Self and Others

Contents

Part II: Organizational Culture

Chapter Six - 65
New Employee Orientation

Chapter Seven - 74
Organizational Culture: Are You in the Right Place at the Right Time for Growth and Success?

Chapter Eight - 85

Tackling the Elephants in the Room:
The Truth About Why You Are Not Getting Ahead

Chapter Nine - 98
Enjoy Success and Get Over Stress!

Chapter Ten - 108
Navigating Different Approaches to Managing Change

Chapter Eleven - 116
Your Destination is Ahead on the Right. Use Caution If You Start to Think You Have Arrived.

Acknowledgements 124

Job◆portunity : Your Career GPS

Going

Places

Successfully

In the World of Work

Preface - The journey begins...

The idea for this book began when I identified a global, human need – parents and loved ones coming home from work stressed, frustrated and concerned about the future state of their careers. I made this discovery as a child. A child witnessing what she perceived as human suffering is pretty devastating. I would get angry or sad about the way I felt my parents were being treated at work. I wanted desperately to help them but at the time I felt there was not much I could do. For me, this global need was painfully discovered through the eyes of a child, I believe it is valid because this discovery was pure and unbiased.
Fast forward 30 years, I can now say I have made a significant impact in relieving this form of human suffering. In my career as a Leadership and Organizational Development Practitioner, it has been my mission to relieve the human suffering that occurs on the job. If you have been a prisoner to your career, my prayer is that this book will set you free. I have worked with thousands of clients in hundreds of companies around the world and yet there are some very consistent and classic scenarios that play out every day, everywhere I go. These consistent experiences over time serve as validation that this book will help YOU. I deliver many of these messages on a weekly basis in individual coaching sessions and collectively in team development sessions.

You have a Job◆portunity which is defined as the chance to make your job an opportunity to achieve your goals and dreams. It is up to you to go beyond having a job and create Job◆portunities for the rest of your career. Use this book to guide yourself strategically throughout the remainder of your career. The impact on your whole life, not just your work life, will be tremendous.

GPS Voice Command: "Continue on this road for 100 miles."

I was inspired to study the science of Industrial and Organizational Psychology with the goal of one day being able to transform the workplace and ultimately change the quality of life for families all for the better. It has been a long road and

I still have quite a distance to travel but the cause is too worthy for me to take a detour.

GPS Voice Command: "In one mile make a right turn on Field of Dreams Avenue."

I finished graduate school with a Master's in Industrial and Organizational Psychology and entered the workplace as an Organizational Development Consultant determined to take on the work world one consult at a time. I am proud to say that my energy and zeal are still at an all time high. However, I now have wisdom and experience to support and sustain my passion for this work.

GPS Voice Command: "In five miles make a right turn on Reality Street."

Experiencing the overwhelming dynamics of the workplace and joining the masses of those that come home stressed, frustrated and concerned about the future state of their careers gave me a wonderful dose of empathetic reality. The dial calibrating my passion for the work I do easily turned to the maximum setting after just a few years.

GPS Voice Command: "In 500 feet, make a U-turn."

After an eight year career in the trenches, The National Institute of Leadership & Organizational Development, LLC was born. Deciding to leave Corporate America and re-enter as a consultant/business owner was the only choice supported by the belief that a significantly greater impact could be made externally for several organizations compared to the impact on one organization as an internal consultant. The Institute has been in business since 2005 and has impacted organizations worldwide.

GPS Voice Command: "Continue on this road for the duration of your career. Do not exit this highway until you have facilitated a career plan for all lifelong learners. Be persistent. I assure you, your destination is ahead on the right."

This book contains the information, tools and strategies to navigate through challenges and develop successful career plans. Buckle up. This ride will be bumpy. Self assessment and reflection will be required throughout. Be encouraged when you feel uncomfortable with the content as this means an opportunity for development has been identified. Every failure should be followed by a growth spurt. Immediately reference this book when you are struggling in your work life. Be open, be strategic, and be ready to fight for your rightful place among those who successfully prosper in their work lives.

This book is meant for more than just reading. This is a book that must be actively studied. In every chapter you will be given the opportunity to **"Recalculate"** your route to job satisfaction and career success. This will take place in the form of an exercise that will promote critical thinking and a true call to action. Have pencils, pens, highlighters, or tablets (for those techies) on hand for taking notes. Make notes and document your reflections about what you are studying. Chapters also feature a **"Reality Check"** which is designed to give you the bottom line real deal on the subject matter. Finally, each chapter will conclude with **"Turn by Turn Directions"** which will sum up the main points of the chapter and help you think about how the content in each chapter will transfer into the day-to-day work lives of the reader.

Challenges will always present themselves in the journey of your career, so come back to this book as often as you need to. Be assured, this book contains the keys to success. Ultimately, the reader will walk away from this book time after time with a Road Map to the next level of success.

Now, let's go! Our journey awaits.

Part I:

Playing the People Game

Chapter One

Perfecting Your People Skills

Allow people to go on and on and on about their favorite topic and they will love you for life. Be prepared, most people's favorite topic is themselves!

Skill with people is critical for success in life. If you cannot get along with others, and more importantly if you cannot influence others, you are going have a difficult journey in the workplace over the span of your career. Often, we find ourselves believing that our technical skills and talents are more important than our people skills. When we think this way, we are wrong. When people regard you as being rude, arrogant and condescending, your technical skills and talents no longer exist. Your brand becomes consistent with cold and negative attributes.

The good news is developing your people skills requires a desire to care for others and to put their needs first, most of the time. This can all be summed up in one phrase: **humbling yourself**. It is a choice that requires that you put yourself, your needs, your frustration, your fear, your anger, your joy, your elation, and your happiness to the side and support someone else. This is a choice, a simple choice, an intentional act. The reality is many people choose not to humble themselves because of one or more of the following reasons:

- Impatience
- Inflated sense of self
- Self-interest
- Pride

What this "looks like" to others is rudeness or arrogance and what it "feels like" is disrespect. Have you ever been in a situation when you have had to take responsibility for an error you did not make? Have you ever had to perform a task that you believed should have been performed by an individual at a lower level than the level at which you were working? Have you ever quietly remained behind the scenes while someone else took credit for your work? If you said yes, to any of these questions you have actively practiced humbling yourself. Chances are for most who have made the decision to humble themselves, they suffered a loss to later experience great gain.

Humbling Yourself – The Foundation

To humble yourself means to lower your own importance. A humble person is courteous and respectful. A humble person puts others first when it is appropriate and/or **strategic** to do so. A humble person listens very well. People who interact with humble people feel better about themselves when they walk away from those interactions. Consider the following scenarios:

Scenario #1: Redundant Questioning

Reflect on a specific time when someone asked you a question that you believed they should have known the answer to. They may have even asked you the same question 5 times before. How did you respond?

____

____

____

____

Scenario #2: All About Me

Reflect on a specific time when you were with a group of colleagues discussing non-work related topics. Did you dominate the conversation by talking about yourself, your kids or your pets or did you allow others to talk about themselves while you eagerly listened?

____

____

____

____

Scenario #3: Taking an "L" (A Loss)

Reflect on a specific time when you know you communicated a point of information but another co-worker came after you and made the announcement as if your initial communications were not thorough enough. Did you make another announcement stating that you had already communicated this point or did you say nothing, hoping that the audience would recognize that you had already made that announcement?

____

____

____

____

Self Assessment

Now consider how you typically behave when you are engaged in different scenarios like the ones above. Complete the following self-assessment. Be honest with yourself. "Yes" is worth 2 points. "Somewhat" is worth 1 point. "No" is worth 0 points.

Redundant Questioning			
Yes	Somewhat	No	**Action Taken**
			Refuse to answer.
			Respond in an impatient manner.
			Respond with a short remark excluding important details.
			Exhibit inappropriate non-verbal behaviors.
			Internally have negative thoughts about the person asking the question(s).
All About Me			
Yes	Somewhat	No	**Action Taken**
			Bring the conversation back to you every time someone else introduces a new topic.
			Dominate the conversation with details of self (If you respond "Yes", indicate "No" for the 3 remaining items).
			Ignore how others are receiving you and your behavior.
			Exhibit non-verbal behaviors indicating lack of interest in the topic.
			Internally have thoughts of boredom about the topic being discussed.
Taking an "L" (A loss)			
Yes	Somewhat	No	**Action Taken**
			Take your co-worker's announcement personally in terms of that person intending to make you appear incompetent.
			Publically remind your co-worker that you already shared those points of information with the team.
			Privately explain to members of the team that you had already made the announcement.
			Confront your co-worker accusing him or her of trying to make you look bad.
			Restate an announcement your co-worker already made in retaliation of what you feel he or she has done to you.

Total Score: ___________________

The Humble Scale

0---------------------------------15---------------------------30

Remarkably Humble Moderately Humble Proud Ego

If you scored...

0-10 Points **Remarkably Humble** - You consistently practice humble behaviors when interacting with others. Your ability and willingness to make yourself less important than others has a deep and profound impact on how sincere and genuine others perceive you to be.

11-19 Points **Moderately Humble** - Your tendency is to demonstrate a moderate show of humility in terms of promoting your own merits and importance. While you do a good job of consistently putting others first, you may from time to time be impatient with others or even boastful of your own accomplishments. The recommendation is to watch the verbal and non-verbal communications of others very carefully in an effort to pick up on cues that indicate you are turning people off or coming across as abrasive.

20-30 Points **Proud Ego** – You have a strong tendency to be self-interested. Your promotion of self and lack of focus and attention on others causes you to come across as arrogant and egotistical. It is strongly recommended that you make consistent choices to serve others, listen attentively, and allow others to talk about themselves instead of listening to yet another story about you. These choices will take your people skills to the next level over a very short period of time.

If you scored 15 points or less, you typically demonstrate good to great people skills. Reflect in the space below in terms of what allows you to put others first on a consistent basis.

____

____

____

____

If you scored less than 12 points, reflect in the space below in terms of what will you begin to do differently moving forward to improve your skill with people.

____

____

____

____

Applying Your People Skills - When to be Humble

Self promotion certainly has its place. There are times where you have to wave a flag that bears your name on it if you want to be recognized as a valuable contributor. However, applying great people skills requires humble behavior when it is appropriate and/or **strategic** to do so. Consider the following opportunities:

- Influence
- Mutual respect
- Service

Influence

Your ability to affect other people can and will have a direct effect on your performance in the workplace. Influence is needed in order to work effectively on a team, to receive acceptance on a proposal or to just convince your boss that you need an extra day off. If you have ever made a purchase as a result of a sales pitch, commercial or an advertisement, you have been influenced. You were able to see yourself and your needs in the sales pitch, commercial or advertisement. You felt important and that your needs would be met. The organization doing the selling **humbled** themselves to you which resulted in you making the purchase. You have to accomplish this in the workplace when you are attempting to influence others.

Influence is a huge part of leadership. Remember, having direct reports, people that report directly to you, does not make you a leader. In fact, the true mark of a leader is to be followed by people that do not report to you. When you need to influence others, being humble is a very strategic method to employ. Try the following actions:

- Sincerely make an effort to learn more about the people you are leading. Allow people to talk about their favorite topic, themselves.
- Make sure the people you want to influence truly feel heard.
- Reach out to those you want to influence for their perspective.
- Reward and recognize others.

Influencing others will take your career to new heights but you have to make others feel important in order to achieve your goals. You have to be humble if you truly want to be influential.

Mutual Respect
We can all relate to having conflict with others. The conflict can be as simple as disagreeing on an approach to a project or as complex as feeling disrespected by a colleague. If both parties really want to resolve the conflict, the primary goal has to be developing mutual respect. This will require both parties to humble themselves. Typically, both parties will not humble themselves at the same time and one person has to be willing to make the first move. This may require that person to be remarkably humble. Consider the following actions:

- Be the first to apologize or admit error
- State 2-3 reasons you respect your colleague. Cite attributes or what you like about their approach to the problem.
- Listen to your colleague's complaints and determine how you can turn those complaints into an opportunity to solve the problem.

These actions will require sacrifice and humility on your part. Nine times out of ten, however, the respect you show will come right back to you in greater doses than you administered. Remember, it all starts with humbling yourself.

Service
Everyone is required to render service excellence in their career, if and only if they want to have a stellar career. You may be in a customer service role where the obvious job requirement is that you render great customer service. If this is the case, you already know that humbling yourself is imperative.

We are not always aware of the fact that we all report to someone in some way, form or fashion. This chapter focuses on three forms of service, leaders serving their followership, serving peers and other internal departments across boundaries, and serving superiors.

As effective leaders, we must diligently serve those we are leading. Individuals who are viewed as poor leaders are most likely not serving others. Poor leaders are typically consumed with their own agendas, ignoring those individuals who are on the ground floor making it all happen. The lesson is to serve those who you are leading and they will in turn take care of and serve you.

Vying for turf and resources is very classic when it comes to interacting with peers and others areas of the business. Unfortunately, the dynamics associated with this can be very nasty. At some point, someone has to do the right thing. Sharing information, resources and space requires behaving in a humble manner. Do not focus just on what you are giving up. Focus on what you are getting.

Opportunities to render service excellence include:

- Serving and supporting the needs of those you are leading. Leaders have to put their followers first. The captain must go down with the ship.
- Working with peers and across departmental boundaries. Poor communication, turf wars and jockeying for resources can cause real challenges for some. Humbling yourself will once again be required to successfully span these boundaries.
- Meeting the needs of your superiors. This may also require you to humble yourself, especially if you believe their requests or demands are "beneath you". Staying focused on your goals will help you to humble yourself without feeling like you are giving up everything.

People often equate being humble with weakness. This is because these individuals are not employing humble behavior as a strategy for improving relationships which could lead to the derailment of their careers. Behaving in a humble manner builds relationships and progresses careers because behaving in a humble manner **BUILDS TRUST**. Trust is the thread of success running through each chapter of this book. When you build trust you advance everything around you. Congratulations, the concept of behaving in a humble manner is now a very BIG tool in your professional toolkit. Use it wisely.

Turn By Turn Directions

Perfecting Your People Skills

As long as the workplace is filled with people, people skills will be required. Developing your people skills has to become a priority on your list of self-development tasks. This chapter provides a great opportunity to hold up the mirror and truly see where your opportunities lie in terms of working well with others.

Humbling Yourself

The key to developing great people skills is putting others ahead of yourself. Making others feel important, heard and valued is truly the key to your success when it comes to developing relationships. The key is to employ humble behavior strategically. Consider your approach as well as the impact of your behavior when creating a strategy for working with others. He who plants humility usually reaps a greater gain.

The Humble Scale

Where did you fall on the continuum of "Proud Ego", "Moderately Humble" and "Remarkably Humble"? Knowing where you are helps you to get to where you need to be. Again, the recommendation is to employ humble behaviors strategically. This scale is intended to provide the data you need to make strategic decisions.

0-----------------------------15-----------------------------30

Remarkably Humble Moderately Humble Proud Ego

Influence

Influence is the ability to affect others. As we are living in a world of constant change, influence has become a critical success factor that separates winners from losers. This is the reality of how things get done today. Humble behaviors can increase your ability to be influential if you strategically put the right people forward at the right time.

Key behaviors that foster influence include:

- Making an effort to learn more about others.
- Truly listening to others.
- Seeking the perspective of others and placing their perspective above your own.
- Rewarding and recognizing others.

Mutual Respect

Establishing mutual respect is a key foundational building block in any relationship. Restoring mutual respect in the midst of conflict can be tricky but it can be facilitated by employing humble behaviors. The challenge here is being willing to commit to:

- Being the first to apologize or admit error.
- State 2-3 reasons you respect your colleague. Site what you like about their approach to the problem.
- Listening to your colleagues' complaints and determining how you can turn those complaints into an opportunity to solve problems.

For some these actions are bitter pills to swallow. For others, it is easier to be willing to humble themselves. Whether you find it easy or difficult, you must practice humility in order to positively and strategically differentiate yourself from the rest of the pack.

Service

Your superiors, peers and co-workers in general may not always respect you or respect your abilities. This could easily lead to you exhibiting behaviors inconsistent with teamwork and partnership. Stay focused on your goals and humble yourself in the sight of your superiors for ultimate gain. Your superiors will begin to see you in a positive and powerful light. Eventually, you will see a huge return on your investment in terms of responsibilities, opportunities and promotion.

Trust

Trust is required to have effective relationships with others. Behaving in a humble manner **BUILDS TRUST**. A great way to measure your people skills is to determine how readily people trust you. If trust is low, humble yourself. Remember, this is a solid strategy in developing skill with people and relationships that will propel you forward.

Your Road Map

What typically prevents you from humbling yourself in the sight of others? After reflecting on these factors, describe how you will overcome these factors moving forward.

____

____

____

____

List 3 strategic opportunities you have to humble yourself at work. Also include what you hope to gain by humbling yourself.

1. ____
   ____
   ____

2. ____
   ____
   ____

3. ____
   ____
   ____

Chapter Two

Workplace Bullying

Managing conflict effectively leads to enhanced communication, builds authentic trust and improves interpersonal relationships.

Many of us have been bullied in a variety of ways. When we think of bullies, we immediately go back to thoughts of the school playground, stolen lunch money and wedgies. Now as adults, we are seeing bullying behaviors in the workplace. There are different types of bullies and different methods of improving relationships with those we perceive as bullies. It may surprise you that the most effective ways of dealing with bullies require self-reflection and humility. Before we get into strategies for dealing with bullies, let's make sure we are accurate in our definition of the word "bully".

Remember the bully of the school when you were a kid? Chances are this person had two or more of the following attributes:

- **Just Plain Mean**
  - *Cold natured*
  - *Rarely smiles*
  - *Has a mean spirit*
  - *Is disrespectful of others*
- **The Challenger**
  - *Challenges or contests most ideas or suggestions*
  - *Refuses to cooperate for the greater good*
  - *Acts pushy and bull dozes their way around*
- **The Abuser of Power**
  - *Abuses their power (power = age/seniority, size, popularity, etc.)*
  - *Interrogates others aggressively*
  - *Micromanages or "nit picks" at the little things*

All together these attributes spell BULLY.

Recalculate: If you are dealing with someone who possesses one or two of these attributes you may NOT be dealing with a bully. YOU might be the one who is in need of a behavior change. What's really interesting is that you can reflect on this, and by adopting a strategic approach, may resolve the relationship issues that exist between you and the one you thought was a bully.

In all cases of bullying, the bully has the right to receive feedback and you have an obligation to offer feedback. Preview the section in Chapter 8 for Delivering Effective Feedback. It is important to ask the person you perceive as a bully if you can give them feedback. If they say yes, then go ahead and deliver the feedback. If they say no, respect their timing and trust that they will come back to you. Here's a quick preview:

- Set the scene to get everyone on the same page. State the time, place and environment where the incident took place.
- Just the facts! Share factual information and behavior that you observed. Do not share your opinions.
- Communicate the results of the factual information you shared. You may also share how it made you feel.

Delivering one point of feedback may not resolve the bullying behavior instantly. However, delivering feedback consistently is a great way to hold the bully accountable. This will curb the bullying behavior over time. It is also a great idea to document each point of feedback you deliver.

Just Plain Mean

Some people who are perceived as being bullies are very cold natured. Before you slap the label of bully across the forehead of these individuals, consider the following strategies targeted for those who rarely laugh or smile, refuse to make small talk, and resist all positive emotions and/or communications.

Strategies for dealing with perceived bullies:

- **Quietly gravitate towards them.** If you find positive reasons to be around these people, they will eventually find positive reasons to be around you. Be creative. This may be as simple as taking a route that will take you past their workstation or sitting at their table at lunch. Being around them does not mean you have to start a conversation with them. It just means being present. Avoiding these people is not the solution. It will only perpetuate the cold distance between the two of you.

- **Ask them for advice.** Most people who feel they are being utilized as a resource for their expertise will instantly warm up to you. For those individuals that are cold natured, it may take a few attempts to get them to warm up to you, but keep trying and be consistent.

- **Kill them with kindness.** How many times have you heard or tried this old adage. This strategy is tried and true because it is virtually impossible to remain cold when being presented with a smiling face, a nice compliment, or a kind gesture. Again, persistent consistency will be the key.

- What other strategies could you use to improve your relationship with individuals who are "Just Plain Mean"? Think about it and document your reflections.

  ____

  ____

  ____

  ____

Remember, a cold natured person could simply be introverted and pessimistic. These are personality traits that take time to overcome so be patient. With a little work, you can engage these individuals and perhaps building a meaningful relationship that will last a lifetime.

The Challenger

There is an individual who publically shoots down your ideas with the skill of a sniper. Ouch! This sounds like it could be bullying behavior. Or, perhaps you are simply dealing with a personality that challenges everything. If this is the case, leverage their challenger tendencies to benefit your agenda or your causes. Think about what you already know to be true:

- You know that this person is probably going to shoot down your ideas, and feel comfortable doing it, because they have done it before.
- You know that you and this person are not typically aligned when it comes to ideas.

- What else do you know? Think about it and document your reflections.

  ____

  ____

  ____

  ____

  ____

  ____

  ____

Based on what you know, here is what you can do:

- **Anticipate the challenges that are going to come your way and prepare!** First, anticipating that you will be challenged is preparation within itself. Now you don't have to experience shock and awe as you receive the challenges.

- **Secondly, try to anticipate why this person challenges you.** Are you in any way threatening this person? Will your position make this person look bad? Will your suggestion facilitate a change that your "challenger friend" will find worthy of resistance? Are there personal reasons that motivate these challenges?

- **Finally, try to anticipate what specific challenges may be presented and prepare a counter that will be viewed as a win-win for all.** This means that you should come up with a few "If, then, therefore..." statements. For example, prior to your highly anticipated meeting you think: "**<u>If</u>** I suggest we plan an employee appreciation day, **<u>then</u>** the person who always challenges me will say 'we don't have the budget to execute an employee appreciation day.' **<u>Therefore</u>**, I need to identify the resources needed to execute this event before I go into this meeting."

Let's look at a situation where a manager wanted to bring in a leadership consultant to do some training. The manager's boss is **The Challenger**. The manager already knows her boss is going to challenge her request by instructing her to go to HR and have someone internal do the work to save money. The manager will then respond with the following If, Then, Therefore statement: "If we use an outside consultant, then our staff will feel more comfortable opening up since the consultant is a 3rd party neutral facilitator and this will free HR up to work on other things. Therefore, we will conserve resources in HR, create a better learning environment for our participants, and get a better return on our investment." With challengers you have to be prepared.

The Abuser of Power

For some people the perception of possessing power is inebriating. The way people conduct themselves when it comes to title, position, seniority, status, expertise, and even physical height can give others the impression that they are a bully. The bully may be convinced that it is okay for them to act like a dictator, speak rudely to others, send scathing emails, publically undermine others, interrogate others, micromanage, or even make decisions without consulting or informing those the decision will impact the most. Those bullies who abuse their power are totally inconsiderate and find satisfaction in knowing they are "running the show". If you encounter a bully who "gets high" on abusing his or her power, consider the following three techniques designed to effectively allow you to deal with this person.

- **Two spoonfuls of COURAGE** – Let's face it. You are dealing with a dominant personality. You are going to have to be just as bold if not bolder than the bully. In order for you to properly execute the strategies listed previously in this chapter, you are going to have to act courageously. This means when you sense risk or fear you have to confidently move in that direction, not away from it. Overcoming a bully who abuses their power is like training an aggressive dog. You have to be firm, appear dominant, and you have to be consistent. If the bully senses fear they will continue to dominate you. **Reality Check:** Without courage, you will not stand a chance against this type of bully.

- **Fight Power with Power** – You have to form alliances with other people in power. Chances are, most people see the same behaviors you are seeing and are dealing with the same impacts you are dealing with. This includes the powers that be. Often times leaders are waiting for feedback from employees who are dealing with difficult people. The more data points and documentation they have, the more aggressive they can be in their discipline. The assumption here is that you have relationships with individuals who have influence in the organization. If you do not have these relationships in place, you have some serious work to do.

- **Take the Bully's Power!** Remove the bully's power over you by diminishing the impact their behavior has on your emotional state, your work, and ultimately your effectiveness. You control how you react and respond to power plays. Any time you experience negative energy, transform it into an opportunity. For example, if decisions are made that you do not agree with, be persistent in proposing solutions. If the decision is out of your control, trust the system and MOVE ON! In no way should you spend time and energy mourning the loss of what you wanted. Recognize when your thoughts are stuck on negativity and immediately go to a place of peace. For some this will be a spiritual place, for others it may be a place that inspires you. Whatever you do, move on from the negativity that is occupying your thoughts.

  For instances of real-time engagement, put on your poker face. In other words, when you are dealing with a live and in person situation, never let them see you sweat, get upset, or become overwhelmed. The best way to diffuse any situation is to walk away. If walking away is inappropriate pause before responding. Then respond with a question that challenges their position in a neutral manner. Some examples of strategically neutral questions include:

  - Why is this important to you?
  - What will success ultimately look like in this case?
  - How can I best support you?/What can I do for you?

  Or just simply state, "That's interesting..." Remember, rise above the trivial behaviors.

  In summary, you have to take dominion over the **Abuser of Power**. When you take the reins of control by administering courage, forming alliances, and determining how you respond to what is being thrown at you, you are effectively in control of the bullying situation. This technically means you are no longer being bullied. Think about it...

Leverage Those with Position Power to Aid in Your Bullying Situation

There should always be at least one person you can talk with that has influence within your organization. When you decide who to go to, consider a careful and strategic approach. The key here is not to be a tattle tale. Go to the leaders you have identified as potential allies and ask them questions that get them to critically think about the behavior of the bully. (See the sample questions below.)

Sample questions to direct to leaders when shedding light on bullying behavior:

- What were your thoughts on the decision that was made by "the bully" regarding X, Y, & Z?
- How should I respond to this statement that was sent to me in an email?
- In your experience, how have you managed individuals who blame others instead of taking personal responsibility?
- How do you think the staff meeting went yesterday?
- Tell me about a time you had to deal with a difficult person. How did you handle them?
- Describe a time in your career where you felt you did not have the freedom to do your job. How did you cope with that?

If you do this correctly, they will in turn ask you questions about your experiences. Now, you have an opportunity to tell the leader about your challenges. Only spill the beans when you have been asked. Your motives are to have the senior leader use their influence to change the bully's behavior and to get your official license to push back, ask challenging questions, and say "no" to the bully without fear of retaliation. Remember, there is safety in numbers, especially when there is power in the numbers.

All is Fair in Work and War

For the more significant actions you feel are being taken against you, wisdom and skill will be required. You will need wisdom to pick your battles and skill to successfully navigate potential landmines and establish clear boundaries. Hopefully, you will get to a point where the exploding landmines are predictable. When you see one coming diffuse it early or stay away from it. Boundaries are also critical with bullies. They need to be told where the "line" is and they need to be given consequences if they cross the "line". Boundaries can be established by putting the bully on YOUR schedule, responding to emails, voicemails, text messages, etc. when you decide to and only with brief and essential content, and by saying NO. Only fight the battles you believe you can win. Winnable battles will consist of predictable landmines, the proper support from key leaders and team members, and attainable resources. Size up your opponent and the situation before you make this decision. When you beat a bully, the bully no longer exists. A few carefully selected battles that result in "wins" for you will result in diluted power plays moving forward.

Take a Balanced Approach to Bullying

Kindness, persistence, consistency, and humility are all critical tools to use when dealing with bullies. It is also important to add one of the following additional dimensions to each of these critical tools.

- **Kindness** should be coupled with **firmness**. Do not allow your kindness to be misinterpreted as weakness. Be firm and steadfast in your position.
- **Persistence** should be coupled with **knowing when to walk away**. My father always told us growing up, "When you strike oil, stop drilling." Know when you have done all that you can do and be aware of when you have achieved a victory, even if it is a small win.
- **Consistency** should always be supported by **flexibility**. Consistency certainly has its place. However, do not focus so much on being consistent that you miss an opportunity to inject a little variety or start a new on something that would benefit yourself and others.
- **Humility** goes hand in hand with **respect**. In your quest to humble yourself, you should make the request that you be respected. This should be an easy request to grant since you have already put yourself second and deferred to others in some way form or fashion. You should never have to tolerate being disrespected.

Take these tools and use them for good. There is always hope in what feels like a hopeless situation and being bullied is no exception. Just when you think things cannot get any worse, challenge yourself by asking the question, "How am I contributing to this situation?" and "What else can I do to improve this situation?" This mindset will propel you over any and every hurdle in your life and career.

Turn By Turn Directions

Don't be so quick to place the label of bully on others

Some people are in a perpetual state of unhappiness. Others naturally have an angry expression all the time. And some people are just plain mean. It is important to discern the difference and to govern your behavior accordingly. Give them a fair chance to dispel your perceptions by giving them feedback. Review the section of Chapter 8 that spells out how to deliver effective feedback. Ask the individual if now is a good time to give them some feedback. If they say yes, deliver it according to the 5 steps:

1. Clarify the environment, location, time of day, or scenario in which the feedback situation took place.
2. Provide feedback only on things you plainly saw or heard. Do not provide feedback on your evaluation, analysis or thoughts about what happened.
3. Describe the outcomes resulting from the situation/issue/behavior. This can either be success, failure or your feelings associated with the situation.
4. Ask what they believe next steps should be.
5. Determine the best time to revisit this conversation. Remember, this is a process, not a one shot deal.

If they say no, respect their timing. I promise they will come back to you because now you have piqued their curiosity. Most things that are cold can be warmed up. Look at this as a challenge and go for it! Not only will you decrease your stress when it comes to this person but you could actually gain an ally or a friend.

Just Plain Mean

For those individuals that just stare at you with an evil eye or send really mean emails, you may want to consider your own behavior. Slowly begin to gravitate towards that person every time you have an opportunity to do so. Proximity breeds contentment. You can also flatter them by asking them for advice. People feel instant warmth when you honor their expertise. Finally, hit them with the old "kill them with kindness" rule. A kind word, a Christmas present, a warm smile and hello consistently over time will melt the coldest icicle.

The Challenger

With challengers, your job is to get to know them so well that you can anticipate their challenges well in advance of the meeting, conversation or interaction with them. Once you anticipate the challenge, prepare your response with an If, Then, Therefore statement

The Abuser of Power

When dealing with someone who is power-hungry and out of control, you have to be wise, strong and COURAGEOUS. Fear will only derail your efforts in dealing with this type of bully. When you are experiencing fear, remind yourself of what you have to gain, not what you have to lose.

It is also important to build relationships with people who have influence in the organization and preferably over the bully. Don't be a tattle tale. Ask key questions. What will inevitably happen is that the person of influence will be flattered that you are tapping into their wisdom and experience and they will in turn ask you about the current state of your work life with care and concern. Now you tell them, in a professionally neutral manner, what is going on. If you do this well, you will earn a protective force field against the bully.

Take the bully's power! Be strong. Don't sweat the trivial things. For things that are more significant, fight! But pick your battles strategically. Don't ever get in a fight you cannot win. Once you beat the bully, they are no longer a bully. All future incidents should be a fair fight between two worthy adversaries.

Trust

When dealing with a bully you have to trust yourself. Trust that you are capable and competent and worthy enough to handle the bully successfully. Trust that you are strong enough to give the bully feedback. You also have to trust those that you select as allies enough to open up to them about your problems. If you can't trust yourself and trust those with influence in the process of dealing with a bully, you will not be successful. Trust is one of the most significant weapons to use against a bully.

Your Road Map

Think of someone who currently or previously fit the profile of bully in your life. What behaviors make them a bully in your opinion? After reflecting on these behaviors, describe your role in how they have treated you.

____

____

____

____

____

List 3 strategies from this chapter for dealing with current or previous bullies that you feel would be most helpful to you.

1. ____
2. ____
3. ____

What will you do differently now that you have studied this chapter?

1. ____

   ____

   ____

2. ____

   ____

   ____

What will you do differently now that you have studied this chapter (continued)?

3. ____
   ____
   ____

Chapter Three

Creating Career Building Relationships

Stop looking at work relationships as though they are non-essential, casual friendships. Start looking at work relationships as criteria for which you will be judged and hopefully supported.

The television show "Survivor" made "alliances" a household term. In the context of the television show, an alliance is defined as two or more individuals who are committed to doing whatever it takes to keep those individuals within the alliance "in the game." This does NOT mean those who are members of the alliance are friends. In fact, the composition of an alliance can change from episode to episode. Strategic alliances in the workplace often function in the same way. People align themselves with those who can help them with specific objectives. True loyalty and friendship can exist within the workplace. However, one has to accurately discern when, where and why relationships exist before one can accurately discern between a friendship, an alliance and an adversary.

My "Best Friend at Work"

Retention rates tend to be higher when employees have a "best friend" at work. A best friend at work means having someone you can confide in, eat lunch with and bounce ideas off of on a consistent basis. The caution here is to choose well. There are a few pitfalls that need to be on the radar of anyone seeking to have a "best friend" at work.

Pitfall #1

Loose lips sink ships. Entering into inappropriate relationships in search of a best friend can be treacherous. Selecting a best friend who will not betray your confidence is important. Consider the information they share with you. If they are betraying the confidence of others, chances are they will do the same to you. The safe route is to share very personal topics with a friend outside of the workplace. This way you avoid being exposed or judged unfairly.

Pitfall #2

Direct reports as best friends. It is never a good idea to display a best friend relationship with individuals that report to you. The supervisor/manager/leader loses credibility and instantly creates an exclusive culture. It is also important to remember the direct report is in a subordinate role so they may feel pressured to comply with any favors or request you ask of them. This could come back to severely haunt you in the form of harassment if the relationship turns sour.

Pitfall #3

Having too many best friends. It is also not wise to seek out "20+ best friends". Your inner circle should never be that large. Having 20 best friends will inevitably result in leaks in information, feelings of exclusion and sure disappointment playing out of the old adage, "you can never please all of the people all of the time." If you are consumed with making sure that everyone likes you, chances are you are very exhausted and very unsuccessful. Consider why it is so important to you to be liked. Also consider that this desire will typically result in paralysis as you agonize on what to do in certain scenarios in an effort to please everyone. You may also get into trouble when it comes to decision making in terms of demonstrating unethical behavior as your values and morals can become clouded by your desire to be liked.

Scenario: Everybody Loves Nick

Nick is a friendly and outgoing person who really enjoys people. That works out well for him since his job involves interacting with almost everyone in the company including the CEO. Nick loves his job, works hard and is the "go to guy" if you want something done or need to know something. He is a great source for official and unofficial information. He gets his information from valid and reliable colleagues that talk to him freely. Nick doesn't consider his behavior a problem since his intent is to get an accurate version of the story. Recently, Nick was passed over for a promotion because someone told the hiring manager that he is an office gossip. Now Nick wonders if he will be stuck in his current position forever.

Questions for critical thought...

Why is Nick known more for his "gossipy behavior" rather than his performance?

___

___

___

___

What should Nick start to do, stop doing, and continue to do in regards to his behavior?

Start: ___

Stop: ___

Continue: ___

Forming Strategic Alliances

There are superiors and individuals that may exist in your peer group or even your direct reporting relationships that can support or propel you towards your career aspirations. The question now becomes have you tapped into these networks and shared your vision for the future with them? Have you identified those individuals that could potentially influence your career path? Have you connected with them and asked for help? Better yet, have you determined how you can add value to their professional lives? Connecting with a colleague with the intent to mutually serve the advancement of each other's careers is a win-win scenario. Just leave the reality TV dynamic of stabbing others in the back out of this alliance.

Forming strategic alliances outside of your department or division at work carries tremendous benefits including the following:

- You will now have access to an expanded pool of resources and information you may need to do your job.
- You will have visibility into other parts of the organization.

- Other parts of the organization will also have visibility into your skill set and capabilities.
- You will now be able to have a larger vision of the systems that exist in the organization. This could lead to opportunities to initiate and work on special projects which typically leads to career advancement.

Sometimes the office dynamic is such that your boss may block your access to his or her peers and superiors in the organization. If you are not visible in the vertical direction on the organizational chart you will have a difficult time when it comes to getting promoted. Why? Because no one at the influence and decision-making level will know you or your capabilities. Look for opportunities to select a mentor formally or informally. Ask for opportunities to get the perspective of key leaders in the organization on industry trends. Be sure to include your boss as one of the superiors you choose to interview. When you see your superiors in passing, stop them and introduce yourself. Then create an opportunity to interact with them again. The bottom line is this: you have to find a way for your superiors to get to know you professionally. Acceptance that this is just not possible will ultimately derail your career.

My Workplace Adversaries

Whether we like it or not, we are going to have adversaries in the workplace. There are some whose imagination has gotten the best of them and they have become paranoid. Then there are those individuals who really are out for blood. First validate that you really do have an enemy on the prowl. Consider the following:

Their Behavior...

- Are you constantly being pulled into a negative drama by this person?
- Is this person constantly making false accusations against you?
- Do you ever feel supported by this person?

Your Behavior...

- Do you retaliate against this person when you feel wronged?
- Do you discuss this person in a negative light with an inappropriate audience?
- Do you consistently make attempts to collaborate with this person?
- Do your actions demonstrate trust or distrust for this person?

Be honest with yourself: are you part of the problem? Be willing to change your behavior before you expect someone else to change theirs. It is very easy to give in to the temptation to send a flaming hot email instead of taking the high road. Consider yourself and then make your next move strategically. Remember, change starts with ownership.

Once you have validated that you have a true enemy at work, your first goal should be to win this person's respect. If you think that is not an option, think again. If you still think this is not an option it is time for you to build a new strategic alliance. Track and document your "enemy's" attempts to sabotage or derail you and seek advice from your strategic partner, also known as someone who has influence over this person's ultimate success. If your network is limited, this may mean that you seek support from Human Resources. The point is, if you truly have an adversary at work, do something about it. Be smart and do not get pulled down to the level your adversary is operating from. Just remember, doing nothing just may lead to your career derailment.

Trust

Ultimately, trust is critical for the success of any relationship. Examine the relationships you are in at work and determine whether or not the required trust levels are present. If trust is lacking, chances are the motives of those involved in the relationships are not pure. Determining trust levels also helps you to see if a healthy relationship is even realistic. Consider the following points in your individual trust assessments:

- Those who betray confidences cannot be trusted because past behaviors predict future behaviors.
- When your direct report is your best friend at work, you will certainly lose the trust of those observing this relationship as accusations of favoritism and exclusion swirl around in their heads.
- Having 20+ best friends also presents many trust issues as it is impossible to please everyone every time. As soon as someone's expectations are not met they will be disappointed with you which will put them on the road to distrust.

On the other hand trust building can be used as a tool to develop strategic alliances and to win back your workplace adversaries. The dynamic of trust can be used as a rudder to determine direction for your next move. Use it wisely and thoughtfully for trust is truly precious.

Turn By Turn Directions

Best Friends at Work

Employee retention is a real issue for some organizations. Having a "best friend" at work increases the likelihood that an employee will remain with the organization. However, beware of the pitfalls that can go along with having a best friend at work. They can and will derail your career.

Strategic Alliances

Developing strategic alliances is crucial to achieving success in your career. There are many benefits associated with building key relationships with individuals who have influence. Never accept the notion that this cannot be done. Sometimes you may have to be creative and persistent while playing it safe, but you can connect with key business leaders who will in turn help you. Make sure you have something to offer in the relationship as well.

Workplace Adversaries

Those that we believe are our enemies actually may not be our enemies at all. Examine yourself as a means of validating the notion that you have an enemy. Self examination may reveal that you are significantly contributing to the difficulties you are having with your arch nemesis. If you truly are dealing with an adversary, "document, document, document" and form a strategic alliance with someone who can support and/or protect you from this person. If you truly have an enemy in the workplace and you ignore him or her hoping they will go away, they will most likely succeed in derailing your progress or even worse, your career.

Trust

Giving and receiving trust in relationships is a very dynamic process. In some cases you are giving or withholding trust to or from others. In other cases, trust is being given or withheld from you. Furthermore, trust can be used as a tool to develop relationships and to resolve issues you have with others. The key here is to be aware that trust is the issue and to use wisdom when giving, receiving or using trust as a power tool to advance your relationships.

Your Road Map

Reflect on your relationships in the workplace. What are your clear opportunities for establishing new relationships and improving existing relationships?

____

____

____

____

List 3 strategies from this chapter you can immediately apply to strengthen your relationships. In other words, what do you need to start doing?

1. ____
2. ____
3. ____

What do you do really well in terms of establishing and maintaining relationships? In other words, what do you need to continue doing?

1. ____
2. ____
3. ____

Chapter Four

Developing True Self-Awareness

"For if anyone thinks he is something, when he is nothing, he deceives himself."
-Uknown

Do you really know who you are and how you come across to others? Are you able to prevent conflict by understanding your "hot buttons?" What do people really think of your approach to things? Are you someone people truly want to work with and spend time with? Through reflection and critical self-examination, you can begin to explore these questions and develop true self-awareness.

Q. How can you be sure that you are an effective team player and people leader?

A. Self Awareness. Having an accurate picture of yourself will arm you with the data to create effective solutions for your overwhelming challenges. In order to have an accurate picture of yourself, you need to have a high level of **Personal Aptitude**.

Personal Aptitude

Personal Aptitude can be defined as understanding and managing your own behavior, emotions and attitude. Personal Aptitude requires self control. Self control requires that one self monitors their behavior and responses to actions, communications, and behaviors directed towards them. This really counts in those Moments of Truth when you are about to make a decision that can make or break a relationship, your performance/effectiveness, or even your career. In summary, the key elements of having high levels of Personal Aptitude include:

- Knowing what emotions you are experiencing in real time
- Accurately seeing yourself the way other people are seeing you
- Knowing what your strengths and opportunities are related to dealing with stress
- Knowing with accuracy what your default emotion is on a daily basis
- Knowing with certainty what your "hot buttons" are

Personal Aptitude Vignette: Hot Buttons, Cool Response

Bob is a member of a project team that is very visible to senior leaders around the company. The team works well together except for when the team members feel the need to promote themselves rather than promoting the team's objectives. Yesterday Bob and another team member were asked to present the team's current status at a Senior Leader Team Meeting. Bob went into the presentation to present team updates. It quickly became apparent to Bob that his teammate's whole objective was to present himself. His teammate constantly cut Bob off and took credit for work he did not do. The deal breaker for Bob was when his teammate openly corrected a statement Bob made in a very condescending and belittling way. At this point Bob became very angry; however, he did not show it. He deferred to his teammate for a few moments and did a nice job of closing out the presentation. After the meeting, three of the senior leaders commended Bob on his performance during the presentation. Two days later, Bob's co-presenter was asked to step down from the team.

One of Bob's "hot buttons" is activated when he feels he is being treated in a condescending or belittling manner. When Bob perceives that he is being spoken to or treated this way, he strategically avoids conflict and potential derailment by recognizing his physiological cues for anger and frustration (i.e., heat rising in his chest up to his neck and face, etc.). By identifying those cues Bob is able to successfully avoid losing his cool or buckling under pressure. It is very likely that Bob's high levels of Personal Aptitude have been one of his secrets to a successful career.

Social Aptitude

Social Aptitude can be defined as being able to pick up on how other people are feeling and using that awareness to manage relationships with others. High levels of Social Aptitude require intentional observation and intuitiveness. In other words, you have to have enough awareness to be able to see what is not obvious. You have to be able to accurately "read between the lines", and "read the handwriting on the wall". You are keenly aware of the emotions of others in terms of what they are feeling and thinking. From that point you are able to use this data to guide your emotions, thoughts and actions. The keys to having high levels of Social Aptitude include:

- Asking others for feedback on your own behavior

- Accurately understanding your strengths and opportunities for handling daily demands
- Accurately understanding how your own behavior impacts others
- Accurately reads the moods of other people

Social Aptitude Vignette: "Clueless Jane"

Most of Jane's co-workers would describe her in one word, ANNOYING. In this morning's staff meeting, Jane's statements annoyed and offended three co-workers in the span of one hour.

Incident #1

The first incident occurred just before the meeting began when Jane, in the presence of several co-workers, attempted to congratulate another employee Jerry, on his recent graduation from college with his bachelor's degree. Jane's intent was golden. She sincerely wanted to wish this person well. However, when Jane asked, "How does it feel to finally be able to be qualified for your role?" the impact of this question changed Jerry's facial expression from a smile to a blank stare. Jerry responded by saying, "It feels great" and immediately walked away. Thinking nothing of Jerry's response, Jane quickly found her seat to begin the staff meeting.

Incident #2

During the meeting one of Jane's co-worker's asked if someone could cover for her on a project for a few days because she had to take some time to care for her child who was recovering from surgery. Jane, again with the best of intentions immediately raised her hand to volunteer to cover for the co-worker saying, "I feel so sorry for you. I'm so glad I don't have kids. I'll cover for your part of the project. Take as much time as you need." Everyone in the room rolled their eyes while Jane sat back satisfied that she was being a great team player.

Incident #3

Finally, as the meeting wrapped up, Jane's boss asked her to resend him another copy of a document Jane had previously sent to him via email. Apparently, Jane's boss misplaced the file. Jane responded by saying, "Sure, I'll resend the document. But just as a point of feedback, this is the third time I've sent this document to you. We have got to hire better admin support for our fearless leader!" Jane's boss had had enough by this time and responded by asking Jane to meet him in his office later that day. Jane walked away from the meeting with high spirits, patting herself on the back while having no clue that her boss was planning to give her some serious constructive feedback later on that afternoon.

Because of Jane's lack of Social Aptitude, she is well on her way to ruining her career.

Now it is your turn to conduct your own self assessment. The first assessment is for you. The second assessment is for you to give to two other people who know you well. Compare how you rated yourself to how others rated you for true insights on how self aware you really are.

SELF AWARENESS SELF ASSESSMENT

Circle the rating that best describes you. Go with your first response and be true to yourself.

Statement	Very Self-Aware		Self Aware		Not Very Self-Aware
Personal Aptitude					
I know what emotions I am experiencing at any given point in time.	5	4	3	2	1
I believe I see myself as others see me.	5	4	3	2	1
I know how well I deal with stress.	5	4	3	2	1
I know what emotion I typically demonstrate. (i.e., I am predominately happy, sad, irritable, etc.)	5	4	3	2	1
I know exactly what my hot buttons are.	5	4	3	2	1
Social Aptitude					
I regularly seek feedback from others regarding my behavior.	5	4	3	2	1
I know how well I deal with demands from others.	5	4	3	2	1
When I express emotion, I am very aware of the impact of my behavior on others.	5	4	3	2	1
I stop to consider the impact of my emails on the receiver before I hit "send".	5	4	3	2	1
I am good at reading the moods/attitudes of others.	5	4	3	2	1

Scoring: Add each rating to calculate your total overall score. Add each rating per competence to calculate your competence scores.

Total ________

Personal Competence ________ **Social Competence**________

SELF AWARENESS SELF ASSESSMENT

Scoring Key:		
Total Self Awareness: 50 - 40 Very Self-Aware 39-25 Self Aware 24-10 Not Very Self-Aware	Personal Competence 25-20 Great 19-12 Good 11-5 Needs Improvement	Social Competence 25-20 Great 19-12 Good 11-5 Needs Improvement
Reflection: Take a few minutes to reflect on your experience of completing the self assessment. Consider your thoughts, your emotions and your reaction to the questions you responded to. Document your reflections below.		
Based on this assessment, how self aware are you? Are you stronger in personal or social competence?		
Take a few minutes to document YOUR greatest leadership challenge pertaining to self awareness.		

The assessment on the following page has been designed for you to gather feedback from others around your Personal and Social Aptitudes. Be sure to select raters who will be totally honest with you. Compare their responses with your self assessment responses.

SELF AWARENESS MULTI-RATER ASSESSMENT

Circle the rating that best describes the person you are rating.

Statement	Very Self-Aware		Self Aware		Not Very Self-Aware
Personal Aptitude					
The person I am rating knows what emotions they are experiencing at any given point in time.	5	4	3	2	1
The person I am rating sees themselves as others see them.	5	4	3	2	1
The person I am rating knows how well he/she deals with stress.	5	4	3	2	1
The person I am rating knows what emotion they typically demonstrate. (i.e., They are predominately happy, sad, irritable, etc.)	5	4	3	2	1
The person I am rating knows exactly what their hot buttons are.	5	4	3	2	1
Social Aptitude					
The person I am rating regularly seeks feedback from others regarding their behavior.	5	4	3	2	1
The person I am rating knows how well they deal with demands from others.	5	4	3	2	1
When the person I am rating expresses emotion, he/she is very aware of the impact of their behavior on others.	5	4	3	2	1
The person I am rating stops to consider the impact of their emails on the receiver before they hit "send".	5	4	3	2	1
The person I am rating is good at reading the moods/attitudes of others.	5	4	3	2	1

Scoring: Add each rating to calculate the total overall score. Add each rating per competence to calculate each competence score.

Total ________

Personal Competence ________ **Social Competence** ________

Scoring Key:		
Total Self Awareness: 50 - 40 Very Self-Aware 39 - 25 Self Aware 24 - 10 Not Very Self-Aware	**Personal Competence** 25 - 20 Great 19 - 12 Good 11 - 5 Needs Improvement	**Social Competence** 25 - 20 Great 19 - 12 Good 11 - 5 Needs Improvement

Becoming more self aware is a critical step in developing people skills and ultimately having a successful career. People want to be around people they like. People want to work with people they like. People want to help promote people they like. Decide what your biggest challenge is, make the corrections and find comfort in the fact that you are developing yourself as a leader. This will inevitably be an uncomfortable process. Find comfort in knowing that discomfort = development . Move forward and make progress through honest self-assessment and being open to honest and sincere feedback.

This chapter challenges you to hold up the mirror and take a hard look at who you really are and how your emotions, thoughts and behavior impact others. This chapter also challenges you to identify one or two people that you **trust** to give you honest feedback about your levels of self awareness. Trusting people to give you feedback also requires that you trust the actual feedback you receive. Trusting this feedback does not mean you have to enjoy receiving the feedback. What it means is that you trust that these people are truly devoted to helping you develop as a person and as a professional. It means that they care enough about you to tell you their truth. You have to trust that this is truly the case. If you can put your disagreement, discomfort, and hurt feelings to the side and put trust in the forefront, you will go further than you ever dreamed you could.

Turn By Turn Directions

Self-Awareness

Understanding self opens the door to understanding others and the environment in which we all exist. This is something we should never take for granted, especially in the workplace. Constantly seeking to understand how and why you think and feel the way you do will enhance the way you are received by others.

Personal Aptitude

At some point, your personal aptitude must become predictable. In other words, you should eventually get to a point where you know how you are going to respond to certain people, behaviors and actions. Being able to predict these responses coupled with knowing and understanding your emotions in real time = high levels of Personal Aptitude.

Social Aptitude

Picking up on the vibe in the room is a skill. Doing something about the vibe that you have accurately picked up on is a choice. Social aptitude is all about developing your skill to be intuitive and choosing to improve the overall situation for optimal results. If you can focus on the fact that there is more than meets the eye and look deeper at what is truly going on with people, you will open up opportunities to build deeper relationships and increase your effectiveness.

Self/Multi-Rater Assessments

It takes courage to assess yourself and allow other people to assess you. Telling yourself the truth may be just as hard as hearing the truth from others. Be of good courage and engage in this level of feedback as often as you can. This is a sure way to keep your levels of self-awareness where they need to be in order to make accurate and positive impacts on others. The bonus here is that you will also earn respect and appear more credible to others.

Trust

There has to be a strong element of trust to say what needs to be said and to hear what needs to be heard. The journey to maintaining self-awareness requires trust. You have to trust yourself to truly be open to what is in front of you. You also have to trust those who are offering you feedback so that the constructive aspects of their feedback can truly transform your mind and your actions. Development requires trust. A child has to trust his or her parent or guardian in order to develop in a healthy manner. An athlete has to trust his or her coach in order to develop and perform at world class levels. Who do you need to trust in order to develop as a professional? Think about it and act on it, TODAY!

Your Road Map

What has been your biggest "Ah-ha" regarding your own self awareness?

____

____

____

List two commitments you are willing make to improve your Personal Aptitude.

1. ____
2. ____

List two commitments you are willing make to improve your Social Aptitude.

1. ____
2. ____

List three individuals/resources you can trust to give you honest and constructive feedback on your behavior.

1. ____
2. ____
3. ____

Chapter Five

Achieving Emotional Synergy with Self and Others

If you live long enough you will face trials. The beauty comes after you emerge from those trials wiser, stronger and more connected to others.

By now you probably have come to the conclusion that the term "work-life balance" is a joke. What is not funny is the stress and tension that goes with managing everyone and everything you have on your plate. Juggling competing priorities and personalities at work with the demands of home may seem impossible on most days. The reality is your work life WILL spill over into your home life and your home life WILL spill over into your work life. Meanwhile, your emotional self is all over the place at any given time. This chapter focuses on how to achieve "work life synergy" and become a more resilient professional.

Q. How can you be more resilient with the goal of managing everything while being productive, effective and creative?

A. The following three actions are required for work life resiliency:

- Reset expectations
- Create a focus that always brings you back to what you love
- Leverage your network for support

The objective of this chapter is to inspire strategies for synergizing the relationship between work and life outside of work. Stress and feelings of being overwhelmed can be reconciled in a manner that is mutually beneficial for the parts of life that pertain to career, home, self and community. Finding these synergies will result in less stress and more resiliency. Achieving this measure will only enhance the whole quality of life, not just parts of life.

Resetting Expectations for Resilience: Turning Disappointments into Opportunities

A major stressor that we can all relate to is disappointment. Feelings of disappointment are universal when it comes to home, work, community and yes, even self. The truth of the matter is when you experience feelings of disappointment it is actually your fault. We are only disappointed when our expectations are not met or exceeded. Think about it.

- You become disappointed with your spouse because you expected him or her to help you keep the house clean.
- You become disappointed with your children because you expect them to behave while in school.
- You are frequently disappointed with your community leaders because you expect them to make decisions in your best interest.
- You are often disappointed with your boss because you expect him or her to support your career aspirations.
- You are consistently disappointed with yourself because you expect to follow what should be a realistic workout schedule.

The expectations outlined above are not themselves unrealistic. However, disappointment enters because the expectations you have set for yourself or others under those circumstances are unrealistic. We unconsciously set these expectations and then are devastated when they are not fulfilled. The key to resiliency and work life synergy is to be conscious in setting expectations. For a while you will be resetting expectations in response to disappointment. However, eventually you will begin a proactive process of setting expectations that are realistic for the person and circumstances involved.

The Link Between Action Oriented Strategic Thinking and Resiliency
In considering the above examples of instances when we all most likely have experienced disappointment and negative stress, how do you typically respond? The following paragraphs provide you with a new way to be resilient through disappointment. The common thread through all of the examples below is taking an action-oriented approach to gaining healthy resiliency. Within the action orientation, there are key elements of strategic thinking applied as well. This will be illustrated by applying remedies that require the action-taker to consider what

success could ultimately look like. The result is that you become more resilient and less stressed because you are now an owner of an empowering strategy.

- If you know your spouse is not in any way form or fashion a neat freak, why would you consistently expect him to keep the house clean? Get over it. Instead of being disappointed and complaining, request that your spouse clean one room today. Notice I said today. Tomorrow you will likely have to make the same request again. Patience and humor is where you will find resilience in this scenario, not disappointment.

- Every child is different and no mother has an ugly baby. In other words, you should not apply the same approach to discipline or even support for every child. Additionally, we all think our children are wonderful and beautiful and to a certain extent, most parents cannot entirely see their child objectively. That being said, you should know your child well enough to accurately set expectations around his or her behavior. If you have a child that runs into a bit of trouble once a month or even once a week, you should not be disappointed. You should expect this, especially if you are not proactively doing anything to strongly encourage the child to change his or behavior. Even if you have children who "never get into trouble" kids will be kids and sooner or later they will have a slight fall from grace. Remember the old saying, "If the student has not learned, the teacher has not taught." Barring any mental or physical diagnosis, you should look at these incidents as an opportunity for you to be a better teacher. And not only that, you should look at these incidences as opportunities for you to be longsuffering concerning your child and his or her behavior. Instead of disappointment, every time your child gets in trouble at school look at the situation, identify any recurring patterns or themes, and decide what commitment(s) you are going to make to change your approach as a teacher and leader in the child's life.

- Community leaders are elected by the general public for a variety of reasons. However, most individuals vote for the candidate they like and whose platform most closely aligns with their values and beliefs. We become disappointed when decisions are made on our behalf that "cost" us a great deal. We want to reap benefits and not assume any costs to our values or wallets. Instead of complaining, take action. Get involved in the way things are run. You can do this at a high level in terms of running for office yourself if you are so inspired to do so. You can get involved moderately by writing and calling your elected officials to convey your thoughts and feedback on the issues. You can also encourage others to do so. There are other opportunities for you to be passively active as well by simply changing the way you vote. The point is to turn your passionate disappointment into progressive action and accept that there will always be a need for you to do so.

- Your boss should be focused on developing you as an employee. You should expect your boss to take an active role in your development. When you realize your boss is not meeting this expectation, your immediate reaction may be to shut down and move into a mode of compliance, otherwise known as "checking the box". Instead of being disappointed with your boss, you should be disappointed with yourself. It is your job to engage your boss as a resource for your development. You should never passively wait for your boss to develop you. You should incorporate your boss into your plan to develop yourself. Decide what you want from your boss and determine how you should go about getting it. Additionally, it is critical that you engage your boss in developmental dialogues once a month. This can be as a mentor or advisor, a subject matter expert, a broker or connector, or as someone who can provide specific feedback.

- You are disappointed with yourself because you are not exercising at the frequency that you know you should be exercising. The problem with your disappointment is that typically, at the start of each day, we know whether or not we are setting ourselves up to be successful in meeting the expectations of our exercise schedule. It is typically not a shock at the end of the day when we realized we have not worked out. If you are shocked, this is not typical and most likely this is the only workout you have missed this week. In this case, you are simply being too hard on yourself. But for those who normally miss more than 3 workouts in a week, your disappointment should be substituted with the reality check that you never really intended to exercise. The question now becomes, who are you attempting to deceive, yourself or others? Next is a realization that you are really disappointed with the fact that you are engaging in this level of deception. Be honest with yourself and others from the start and your disappointment will fade away with your deception.

Disappointment due to unmet expectations will inevitably compound the issue contributing to your lack of work life synergy. In fact, a significant factor in you not being able to handle everything that is on your plate at work and at home is in large part due to the negative emotions you experience on a day to day basis. In order to keep your emotions in check and ultimately be more resilient, it is imperative that you lean on the examples above. Consider them when creating an approach to resolving emotion filled issues related to disappointment and other negative stressors.

Create a Focus on What you Love

When your energy levels are totally zapped and you feel like the walls are caving in, create a new focus. You have to force your thoughts, your language and your actions to focus on what you truly love. This can be as simple as looking at a photograph on your cell phone or as complex as taking a moment to play the piano or go for a run. The amount of time it takes to refocus your entire being on what you love is irrelevant. What is relevant is that you have the presence of mind to realize that you are in a moment that requires refocus. You have to be conscious and aware that you are experiencing this "Moment of Truth". Some examples of "Moments of Truth" that require refocus may include:

- Participation in a stressful meeting
- Working on a difficult project
- Dealing with a difficult person
- Showing up late for a meeting
- Making a presentation after arguing with your spouse
- Missing an important family event
- Dealing with crying children
- Dealing with a sick or injured child
- Managing financial challenges

When you are in these moments, it is important to remember that you cannot stay in the stress that goes along with these moments. You have to take your thoughts, language and actions to another place. Decide what your focus will be and stay focused on what you truly love. Not only will this give you a renewed sense of energy, but you will also be able to resolve the challenge with a greater sense of clarity and wisdom.

Leverage Your Network for Support

A critical component of resilience is getting support from others. Sometimes you need to talk to someone. Other times you need advice. At other times you need for others to actually step in and do something on your behalf such as connecting you with others. The important lesson here is to be courageous enough to ask for help. Asking for help "looks like" seeking others out for advice or action. If you feel vulnerable when doing so, embrace those feelings because this is a clear sign that you are on the road to resiliency. Asking for help does not have to mean that you are incompetent or incapable of performing. It means you are resourceful enough to leverage your relationships and confident enough to open yourself to other perspectives. Good relationships, professional or personal, should bear fruit. Look at leveraging your network as your opportunity to finally eat the fruit you have been working so hard to grow through developing relationships with others.

The only word of caution concerning leveraging your network is to be careful who you choose to confide in. When you confide in someone professionally, understand that the information you share will reflect on you as a professional and may even be shared with others in the organization. Because of this, be selective as to who you talk to as you never know how something innocently shared can impact your career. When you confide in someone personally regarding work related matters, make sure your confidant has enough relevant knowledge to be helpful if you are looking for insights and pearls of wisdom.

Just Get Over It!: The Direct Path to Resiliency

"A fool shows his annoyance at once, but a prudent man overlooks an insult."
Proverbs 12:16 NIV

We are all guilty of taking a problem that has been presented to us and making more out of it than we should, holding on to it for far too long, and taking it out on those that we should not take it out on. In short, we have all been guilty of contributing to our own stress and feelings of being extremely overwhelmed. There are instances that warrant all of the drama that comes with it. However, there are many instances where we could **choose** to just get over it. Getting over it is truly a choice but for some reason we often cannot see it as one. We force ourselves to dwell in the drama of our situations at times, but we do not have to dwell there. The skill here is to learn to discern between those stressors and areas of disappointment that truly need an action-oriented strategic approach and those that we just need to get over.

The other piece of this is that when we do become disappointed and overwhelmed that we not expose our fragile state to others. If you consistently show your annoyance, you will send the message that you do not handle pressure well, you do not play with others well, and that you are only truly functional when things are going your way. This is not the picture you want to paint so try to use your professional poker face when you know that you are going into a situation that is potentially stressful.

The point of this chapter is to substitute your disappointment with action. The common denominator in this chapter is trust. Trusting yourself to establish realistic expectations and trusting yourself to move out of your so-called disappointment into a mode of action oriented strategic thinking that is laced with passion and truth telling. If you can trust yourself to see the reality in front of you and to do something about it, you will overcome your disappointment of self and others in a rapid and constructive manner.

Turn By Turn Directions

Achieving Work Life Synergy & Resiliency

Most people will confirm the fact that there is no such thing as work-life balance. However, it is a very realistic goal to achieve synergy in our lives. It is important to remember to reset expectations, create a focus that always brings you back to what you love, and to leverage your network for support. Be creative and thoughtful and do what works for you. Getting back up again will become a way of life for you. In fact, practicing resliency will actually lead to taking a proactive approach to problem solving rather than a reactive approach to problem solving. You can do it!

Transforming Unmet Expectations (Disappointments) into Opportunities

When you experience disappointment that is your cue to take action. You will need to immediately look at the problem through different lenses, and decide what your new and exciting opportunity will be. Positive thinking in the midst of what feels like disappointment and possibly devastation will require the presence of mind to create a new opportunity above and beyond what you originally wanted or decided on. Transformation involves change; overcoming feelings of disappointment is required. Reset those expectations and get on board with new concepts.

Action-Oriented Strategic Thinking

Now that your mind is ready to change and create, it is time to take action. Is there anything worse than being disappointed and doing nothing about it? Yes, being disappointed and taking action that is not thoughtful almost always leads to further disappointment. Positive energy has to be channeled into strategic purpose. Consider what success should look like as well as the potential side effects and direct effects of what you are looking to create. Movement in a strategic manner is the key to achieving resiliency. Failure to do this will further promote stress.

Just Get Over It!

Simplify. Sometimes you just have to move on. That's it. Try it! It is very liberating.

Trust

Resilience is all about getting back up again to move forward after a setback. This requires that you find a certain level of resolution and or peace with whatever is stressing you out. In order to find that peace, you have to trust that everything within the current state of your world will work together for good. This peace, trust and contentment with the current state of your work world will facilitate your ability to move into a mode of action oriented strategic thinking. Trust, once again, is the key to true progress in your career journey.

Your Road Map

What circumstances typically surround feelings of disappointment for you?

____

____

____

List three individuals that have disappointed you in the last six months. Now draft three strategies you can employ to move from places of disappointment to places of action-oriented strategic thinking in order to improve those relationships.

1. ____
2. ____
3. ____

List three commitments you are willing make regarding not showing your disappointment to others.

1. ____
2. ____
3. ____

Part II:

Organizational Culture

Chapter Six

New Employee Orientation

Every accomplishment starts with a decision to take action and move forward.

Whether you are working in a first job, a new job, or have been in your current role for 10 years, this chapter is for you. Today is the first day of the rest of your career. Today you begin anew. Too many times we find ourselves saying, "I hate this job!", or "I wish I did not have to work!" without realizing how damaging it can be to say or think such negative things. In the preface, I dedicated this book to all the children and families who watch their loved ones endure the stress associated with their jobs. The goal of this chapter is to help you, the reader, build new perspectives so that we no longer perpetuate negativity about work. The objective is to change your disposition by changing the way you think and feel about work.

In this chapter you will learn how to:

- Embrace and celebrate the fact that you work.
- Be rated as an excellent performer
- Effectively function as a member of a team

Reflection:

Why do you have a job? Why do you work? What purpose do you REALLY want your job or your work to serve? Think about it and record your thoughts.

____

____

____

____

"Nothing has ever been achieved by the person who says 'It can't be done.'" – Eleanor Roosevelt

It's YOUR Choice

Most people work to meet their family's basic needs. There will always be those that work to "keep up with the Jones'es". Some have found their true calling and work to fulfill their passions. Others work because they are following the "order" of life – finish school and get a job. Regardless of your true motive for working, it is critical that you acknowledge that you are **choosing to work**. Having a career is in fact a choice. You can choose not to work and deal with the consequences. Even if you are unemployed but desire to work, you are still choosing to work in hopes of finding a job soon. The point is, since you are choosing to work, embrace YOUR choice. The alternative is to despise and begrudge your choice to work. Having a negative outlook on work is the best way to set yourself up for failure. You will never reach your true potential and you will never truly be satisfied with your life if you choose not to embrace your career. Embrace your work and make your work your PLAY! The benefits far outweigh the costs.

Your Performance

The best way to embrace and celebrate your choice to work is through excellent performance. Being an excellent performer is not just about working hard. It's about knowing what is expected of you and understanding how to navigate through your work journey in a diplomatic, politically savvy manner. Many are not willing to play politics. In fact, I have heard many people say they are not willing to "Play the Game" at work. I am here to tell you that if you are unwilling to play the game, you are NOT in the game. My advice to you is to get in the game and be an excellent player. Get to know your boss, your peers, and your direct reports. Understand what motivates them as well as what factors promote conflict and distrust. A great evaluation of your performance depends on your ability to play the game.

Being an excellent performer is also about being grateful that you have the ability and opportunity to work. Let's face it, in this economy, we should really be appreciative of our jobs. Also, we need to remember that the recession/depression of 2008 – 2015 is most likely NOT the last recession/depression we will face in our lifetime. Be grateful. Be thankful. Do not take your job for granted. You may not be in the most ideal situation right now but it could be worse, much worse.

In this chapter, it will be especially important for you to "hold up the mirror" and be honest about what you see. Remember, if you do not like what you see, be encouraged. In fact, get excited because you have identified an area for growth!

Poor Performers

Poor performers can be described as those who...

- Speak poorly of the organization or the leadership team
- Use limiting language (i.e., "this is the way we have always done it; this cannot be done, etc.)
- Constantly immerse themselves in negative drama
- Use gossip as their main form of communication
- May be inconsistent in punctuality or attendance
- Are not dependable

Interestingly the above list makes no mention of productivity or technical competence. Poor performers may be extremely productive and highly competent. However, if their behavior destroys the team, is distracting to others, or lowers morale, the individual should be considered a poor performer. Unfortunately, organizations often fail to manage poor performers effectively but a decision has to be made: invest in their development OR exit them from the organization. Often poor performers are allowed to carry on and derail their teams without end. The mismanagement of poor performers often results in the loss of key talent (namely satisfactory and excellent performers) within organizations.

Satisfactory Performers

Satisfactory performers can be described as those who...

- Genuinely want to contribute to the organization
- Complete assignments accurately and on time

- Communicate effectively
- May be involved in negative drama from time to time
- May be inconsistent in punctuality or attendance
- Are valuable to the organization

Satisfactory performers are good contributors and are usually competent. They almost always need skill development in one or more areas, but their contributions to the team and the organization are significantly valuable. From a performance management standpoint, organizations must support the satisfactory performer through rewards, engagement and individual development planning.

Excellent Performers

Excellent performers can be described as those who...
- Are able to influence others
- Communicate effectively across all levels of the organization
- Demonstrate courage
- Take ownership of processes and outcomes
- Practice critical and strategic thinking skills
- Know how to build an effective team
- Apply excellent problem solving skills (and are rarely involved in negative dramas)
- Are consistently present and on time or early
- Have superior technical skills
- Are critical to the organization

Excellent performers are those individuals that the boss can leave in charge and not worry about productivity or quality. They are extremely competent and consistently look to exceed the expectations of their job. From a performance management standpoint, organizations often risk losing their key talent by failing to engage and challenge their excellent performers. When excellent performers feel the potential for growth, learning and promotion are lost they will move on to the next opportunity.

Managing Performance

There are two ways to manage performance. You should start by managing your own performance. How would you honestly classify yourself? Performance is not solely based on productivity or technical expertise and turning in deliverables on time. You can be the best producer in the company but if you are consistently spreading your discontent around the organization, and derailing the dynamics of your team, you are a poor performer. The key is to accurately appraise your performance and create your own development plan for taking your performance to the next level.

The second way is to manage the performance of others. Often times we think we have to be in a supervisory or leadership position to manage performance. This just simply is not true. It is your obligation to support the performance of anyone who holds a stake in your career, projects and work assignments. Keep in mind that at the end of the day it is you who will be responsible for your deliverables, not the 5 other people who you depended on in "the system" to get the job done. There is nothing worse than listening to an individual explain their work failures by throwing someone else under the proverbial bus. That individual should have been managing the performance of his or her scapegoat long before the systems failure occurred.

The best way to manage individuals you do not have direct authority over is to decide how to effectively communicate with them.

- If they are **responsible** for a major portion of your work assignment, you have to work diligently to establish a good relationship with them which includes frequent and varied forms of communication. Your communication plan for this person should also be mutually agreed upon. This will counteract the potential for "dropped balls" and misunderstandings moving forward. Your work sessions have to embody the elements that define respect for all parties. You may require an agenda for all work sessions, others may not. You may view the list of priorities differently than others. Whatever the differences are, it is your job to facilitate buy-in for the greater good in a respectful manner.
- If these individuals possess key points of information that you need to do your job, you have to view them as a **consultant** and treat them

accordingly. Let them know that you are leveraging their expertise. Schedule consults with these individuals in advance and according to the planned stages of the project. They need to know they will be brought in to serve a specific function but will not have involvement in other aspects of the project.

- There are some people that you just need to manage by keeping them informed. They don't need to get in the work trenches with you. They do not need to engage in consultative dialogues, they just want updates. Keeping these individuals informed could be the key to keeping your project funded and supported by key stakeholders.

Consistently practicing the above communication plans is another way to build trust with others. Another significant form of communication is giving and receiving feedback. Chapter 8 of this book will provide you with the skills and tools necessary to give effective feedback. Feedback is the key to developing others which is significant when managing others. This includes your boss or other superiors.

The way you perform, which includes the way you communicate, factors in to whether or not people are going to trust you. Building high trust levels will give you your greatest advantage when it comes to successfully managing all aspects of your work environment.

Turn By Turn Directions

Choosing to Work

Whether or not this is a conscious choice for you, it is still a choice. Embrace it. Setting yourself up for success makes much more sense than setting yourself up for failure. This is a key to synthesizing the content in this book for the greater good of your career journey. Check your motives, your true motives for working. Do you need to recalculate your motives? If so, you will have an opportunity to do so at the end of this chapter. Now, think positive thoughts as you prepare for your next work day. After all, your next work day is the first day of the rest of your life!

Excellent Performers

What type of performance do you demonstrate in the workplace? If you are an excellent performer, focus on your energies on identifying a mentor who can support your quest for excellence and connect you with resources that can help you along your journey. You have to own your development by facilitating the opportunity to be challenged. The sky is the limit as long as you don't get complacent. Excellent performers have been known to slide down to the satisfactory (or worse) performance level.

Satisfactory Performers

Which way do you go? Satisfactory performers are usually steady but there is a greater probability that they will either become excellent performers or poor performers. If you are a satisfactory performer, the two keys for you are to solicit feedback, and to be open and receptive to the feedback. It is very important to know specifically what you do well and what you need to work on. Collaborate with your boss to put an individual development plan together and execute!

Poor Performers

If you are a poor performer, you need to come to terms with the reality that you are a problem. Poor performers are detriments to the team. Most poor performers behave poorly AND produce inaccurate, late, low quality results. However, there is nothing worse than a poor performer whose work is stellar, excellent and superior but whose behavior destroys the team and undermines leadership. As a poor performer, you have a duty to change. If you are not qualified for the role you are in, change roles. If you are a drama king or queen, STOP the madness! If you are horribly unorganized and undisciplined, develop those skills in collaboration with an accountability partner. Take action to correct your performance before action is taken on you.

END

Trust

The way we behave and perform are the fundamental data points others use to decided whether or not they are going to trust us. Imagine a goldfish in a glass fish bowl. No matter where the fish swims, it cannot hide. The fish is being watched at all times, even when it doesn't realize it is being watched. You are the goldfish and your life if the fishbowl. Be mindful of the data you are providing to others. Building trust with others is one of the true cornerstones for success on the journey of your career.

Your Road Map

Indicate your performance level below. Explain your self-rating.

____

____

____

List two strategies or commitments you are willing to make to get you to the next level of performance (if you are a high performer, list strategies to stay there).

1. ______________________________________
    a. Resources Needed:
    ____
    b. Completion Date:
    ____

2. ______________________________________
    a. Resources Needed:
    ____
    b. Completion Date:
    ____

Recalculate: List your NEW top three motives for achieving or maintaining excellent performance.

1. ______________________________________
2. ______________________________________
3. ______________________________________

Chapter Seven

Organizational Culture: Are you in the right place, at the right time for growth and success?

Position yourself in the environment where you can realistically achieve your greatest potential.

Job dissatisfaction and turnover occur for a variety of reasons. Fit is one of them. Do you fit in the culture of the organization you are working within? There are different ways to fit. One is *location fit*. Do you love or hate the city your work in or the location of your workplace? Another is *technical knowledge/competence fit*. Are you qualified to do the job? And then there is ***cultural fit***. Can you truly align your beliefs and values with the way your organization operates? While the first two types of fit are often easier to discern, deciding whether or not you fit culturally can take some observation and reflection.

In this chapter you will learn how to:

- Discern your work values, as well as those of your organization.
- Align your work values with the values that make up the true culture of the organization.

Striking Alignment

What matters most to you at work? Is it a leadership team that "walks their talk?" Does your boss have to be competent in order to earn your respect? Do you need an atmosphere of sincere caring amongst your co-workers? Are flexible work hours critical for you and your family? Do you need to have a best friend at work? Do you need to have fun at work? Does it make you crazy that your co-workers, who are slackers, are never held accountable? All of these concepts can be translated into personal work values. We all have those "deal breakers" that lead directly to your job satisfaction or dissatisfaction. The trick is to align your personal work values with the values of the organization. The **areas of alignment** occur when what is important to you or what you value is the same or similar to what the company values. These areas of alignment should be celebrated and strengthened. Think about how you can leverage these areas in terms of your contributions to your boss, your co-workers and the organization as a whole.

When what you value is different from what the company values, this is what is known as a **gap** or a "need." Once you identify gaps, your responsibility is to take the necessary steps to close those gaps. Please note this is YOUR responsibility. It is not the responsibility of your boss, your co-workers or the organization you work for. It is yours and yours alone. Why? Because this is YOUR life and YOUR career; now take charge of it!

Identifying Areas of Alignment and Gaps

So how do you determine the true values of the organization? Do not simply go to your company's website and read the list of values that correspond with the company's vision and mission statements. Do seek to understand what drives your organization's culture. In other words, define the culture, or the way things are done. As you work through the following exercise, think about critical incidents that have occurred in the past, decisions that have been made, and actions that have been taken that have had an impact on you, your team and the organization as a whole.

GPS Voice Command: "Recalculating"

Indicate what is most important to you, as well as what you believe is most important to your organization regarding the following themes:

My Work Values	My Organization's Values
Leader Behaviors • __________ • __________ • __________	**Leader Behaviors** • __________ • __________ • __________
Diversity • __________ • __________ • __________	**Diversity** • __________ • __________ • __________
Worklife Balance • __________ • __________ • __________	**Worklife Balance** • __________ • __________ • __________
Relationships at Work • __________ • __________ • __________	**Relationships at Work** • __________ • __________ • __________
Managing Performance • __________ • __________ • __________	**Managing Performance** • __________ • __________ • __________
Social Events/Interactions • __________ • __________ • __________	**Social Events/Interactions** • __________ • __________ • __________
Technical Skill/Competence • __________ • __________ • __________	**Technical Skill/Competence** • __________ • __________ • __________
Policies & Procedures • __________ • __________ • __________	**Policies & Procedures** • __________ • __________ • __________

Closing the Gaps

For those areas you have identified as gaps, take a minute to decide if they are negotiable. In other words, can you "live with" the values of the organization OR does something have to change in order for you to function effectively in your current role or organization? If you can "live with" the gap, you now have the advantage of awareness. You are aware that your values are not necessarily consistent with those of the organization. This will give you valuable insight into sources of frustration, conflict and confusion moving forward. Use these insights intentionally to make decisions that will support your career.

Are you on the right bus?

For those values gaps that you cannot "live with", be realistic about how likely they are to ever change. Please note that realistic and pessimistic are two different things. The reality is many things can change when the right approach is applied. However, in many cases the reality is that they will not. So be realistic in your view of the gaps you cannot "live with". If there are more of these than areas of alignment, you may be in the wrong place at the wrong time in your career. **Reality Check:** Do you need to leave your current position and/or your current organization in search of a better fit? For some, this will be a harsh reality. For others, this will be a relief that what they knew all along is that it is time to move on. Change can be difficult but if the process of change does not challenge you and cause you a bit of discomfort, you will not grow and your situation will not improve.

Influence

For those gaps that you deem realistic prospects for change, you will have to become a facilitator of the change you need. In other words, you have to become a leader who has influence. **Influence** can be defined as effecting the actions, opinions or behavior of others. A true leader is able to influence others without having to have authority or position power. You don't have to be the boss to have influence. You do have to engage others to the point where they want to follow your lead. If you believe you are not in a position to influence others because your title does not carry enough weight, you are wrong. You CAN influence others at any level by strategically working through people to get the decision maker(s) to sign on to the new way of doing things.

The first step in becoming a leader with influence in an effort to close the values gaps is to identify the source of those gaps. Potential sources could be:

- Your boss
- Your peers
- Your direct reports (those who report to you)
- Leadership in other areas of the organization
- The culture
- The rules/policies/procedures
- The way things have always been done
- Resources
- Budget
- Your work schedule
- Unrealistic expectations
- Others? ___________________________

Find the source and begin brainstorming creative, strategic alternatives to the current state. The key to closing gaps and being a facilitator of change is to remember no matter what industry or job function you are in, ultimately you are in **SALES**. It is your responsibility to facilitate change by recommending improvements, resolving challenges and closing the deal. Facilitating change requires that others adopt a willingness to turn away from the old and turn to the new. There has to be a discomfort or dissatisfaction with the old way of doing things and a bright shiny value in turning towards the new. When you purchase something significant, there is often an emotional connection whether it be excitement with the new or disappointment with the old. When you sell your approach or ideas, you will have to inject the appropriate emotions using your powers of persuasion and enlightenment. Employ the following keys to selling and you will see more alignment between your values and the values of the organization you work for.

"Never doubt that a small group of committed people can change the world. Indeed, it is the only thing that ever has." -Margaret Mead

Keys to Selling:

- Identify the source of the gaps.
- Assess your relationship with that source. Do you have influence there? If so, leverage the relationship. If not, make connections with someone who does.
- Besides the source of the gap, is there a decision-maker involved in closing the gap?
- Assess your relationship with that decision maker. Do you have influence there? If so, leverage the relationship. If not, make connections with someone who does.
- Sell, don't tell. Ask thoughtful, open-ended questions that result in deep discussion.
- Support your position with objective data, not hopes, dreams and feelings.
- Anticipate objections and be ready to overcome them.
- Do not give up if you are passionate about the gap. Get at least three "NO's" before you hit the pause button, change your approach or your position.

If you are of the personality type that needs a written plan for this, consider drafting an approach document. This document will contain the following information:

- Purpose
- Description of the gap and the recommended solution (the issue or process in need of change)
- Details on the approach and methods of developing and implementing the solution
- The Value Proposition or Business Case
- Metrics to evaluate progress
- Success Criteria (what success will look like)
- Timeline

Your focus can now be strategy and execution. You should no longer be mired in the misery of the gap itself. Make this your mission and put some energy behind it. And remember, no man is an island. Work through others to get the job done. This is an excellent opportunity to expand your network. Now let's focus on those relationships that you will need to have in place to make this and other interactions successful.

"People do business with people they know, like and trust." – Unknown

Remember, everyone who has a job and wants to be successful is in sales whether they like it or not. One of the most important elements in the psychology of sales is that people will buy things from people they know, like and **trust**. The best way to embark upon getting people to know, like and trust you is to show **support** for them in the way they would like you to support them. Notice, I did not say support them in the way YOU would like to support them.

Consider this scenario: You are working on a project team. After a month of hard work, the team produces an exceptionally excellent deliverable. However, due to constant conflict, poor communication, and negativity, your teammates complain that they ***never*** want to work with you again. Can you, your contributions, and ultimately your performance be considered successful?

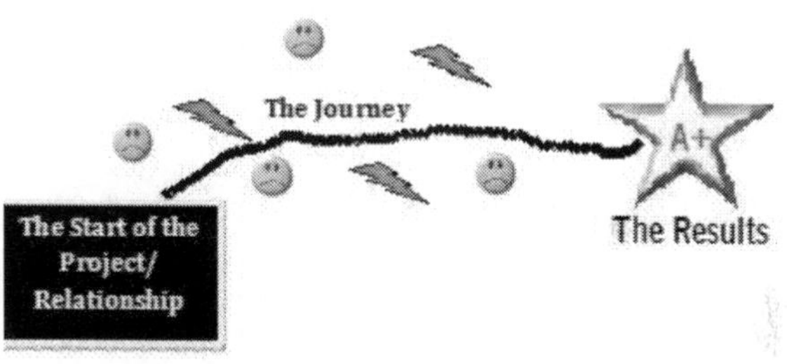

The answer is no. Your focus has to be on people, not just process and outcomes. A focus on people is always going to get you to a place of true success. This concept holds true for organizations as a whole as well. Most departments, sectors, divisions or enterprises produce excellent results. But if you really look at the journey to those results you will find strife, conflict, broken partnerships an broken trust. The bottom line is support the humanistic aspect of the process.

So, how do you determine how others want to be supported? The answer to this question is very simple as well as two-fold. First, you ask them. You can phrase this question in a variety of different ways:

- How can I support you as your teammate?
- Do you have everything you need to do your job?
- Do you have any questions?

Second, be ready to deliver on these questions. The fastest way to destroy trust and ruin your credibility is to ask these questions and fail to follow through. Do not ask if you are not sincerely ready to support others.

Turn By Turn Directions

Work Values: Gaps vs. Areas of Alignment

When individuals agree to take a job, they are entering into a psychological contract with their employer. This contract is not written, it is understood. There are certain things the employee expects of the employer and there are certain things the employer expects of their employee. As long as the contract is in place the employee is satisfied and the employer believes a good selection decision has been made. However, when one party feels the psychological contract has been broken, the first place to look is to work values. An accurate assessment of where the psychological contract has been breached can be traced back to the gaps between the employee's work values and the values of the organization. Strengthening those areas of alignment and closing the gaps is the key to reestablishing the critical psychological contract.

Leadership Influence

Closing gaps and facilitating change requires leadership influence. Title is not important when it comes to influencing others. What is more important is that you identify the sources of the gaps and the decision-makers who can truly affect change. Once you have successfully done this, you can strategically work through others to facilitate change.

Sales

Everyone who is successful in his or her career has been successful in sales. It does not matter what industry or job function you are in. Sales has to be at the center of your approach to leading others and facilitating change. Successful people are effectively able to engage others emotionally and trigger decisions required to facilitate change. Asking open-ended questions, producing data driven results, overcoming objections, demonstrating passion for your position are the keys to successful selling.

Support

Over time, the journey is more important than the results. It is important to support others in the way they need to be supported, not in the way we choose to offer support. At the end of the day it does not matter how many shiny, glittering products you produce if no one wants to work side by side with you. You want to be an asset to the team, not a detriment.
Offering strategically placed support could literally save your career and move you to the next level.

Trust

Offering support for others is also an excellent way to build trust. Another way to build trust is to do what you say you are going to do. Be a man or a woman of your word. If you ask a question, be ready to do whatever it takes to respond to the answer. If the answer to your questions is not feasible or realistic, be honest and give fast feedback along with the opportunity to keep brainstorming until the solution becomes more practical. This is the recipe for becoming a trustworthy, credible leader.

Your Road Map

Describe the most beneficial concepts you learned as a result of studying this chapter. Explain why you found these concepts applicable in your work life.

____

____

____

____

Considering a current challenge you are having, list two strategies or commitments you are willing make as a result of studying this chapter.

1. ____
2. ____

List three individuals/resources you need to now engage as a result of studying this chapter.

1. ____
2. ____
3. ____

Chapter Eight

Tackling the Elephants in the Room: The Truth about Why You are not Getting Ahead

Fear

Do not be afraid to be successful. Drive FEAR out of your heart and mind and embrace your potential.

"Drive out fear." – W. Edwards Deming

There are three "elephants in the room" – issues that everyone notices but no one talks about - that must be tackled before we can move forward. I refer to them as the "Three F's": Fear, Feedback and Finger Pointing.

Fear is a powerful force in the workplace. It keeps people from saying what needs to be said and from being who they really are. Fear paralyzes people and keeps them from realizing their full potential. The major sources of fear in the workplace include:

- Ineffective communication
- The unknown
- Change
- Personality
- Workplace Bullies
- Any type of loss

Ineffective Communication

The absence of good information always leads to speculation and gossip. That is correct, most of the speculation and gossip in the workplace is driven by fear. The problem with this is the level of accuracy associated with the speculation and gossip. If you do not have access to the information you need, you have to ask yourself why. Here are a few "maybe's" for you to consider:

Maybe it is not time for you to access this information. Timing is everything. Finding out something too soon could have a negative impact. Ask yourself if you need to be more patient rather than allowing fear to drive negative communications such as complaints and gossip.

Maybe you cannot handle the information. Think about it. The President of the United States does not hold a press conference and tell the American people classified information. Why? For our safety and security primarily. But also because we cannot handle it. If we knew even a tenth of what threatens our world as we know it, we would buy all the bread and canned goods in the grocery store and live in underground bunkers. The same holds true for our children. We do not share health concerns or financial problems with them because emotionally, they cannot handle the information. Now, compare this to your situation at work. Leadership and employment levels exist because, ideally, these levels allow information to flow in a manner that supports the execution of workflow. The issues and information the CEO of a major corporation deals with are not the same issues and information that a front-line employee deals with. At some point you have to trust that the system has been designed to support you in your role.

Maybe the intentions of the sender were not understood by the receiver resulting in negative outcomes. When something rubs you the wrong way, seek to understand before you draw negative conclusions. If you take the time to discover what the sender's true intentions are, you will have greater clarity. Remember, your behavior is going to be based on your understanding so seek to understand before you respond.

Maybe you should ask. If you do not have all the information you need, it is your responsibility to seek out the information. Sometimes the information has bottlenecked at a certain level of the organization because no one pulled the cork by simply asking. We all get caught up in our competing priorities and unfortunately communication is not always a priority for leaders. Ask the question before you decide to make up stories and spread your discontent in a viral manner. The key to asking is to listen carefully to the answer. In the act of listening you can ask clarifying questions or you can be content with what you heard.

At any rate, do not allow the lack of good or sufficient information to make you fearful. You have the power to control how you respond to ineffective communication.

The Unknown

Death is the great unknown and most people fear death. Some of the great unknowns at work are layoffs, pay raises, promotions, disciplinary action, retaliation, a new boss, or a new system for workflow. Sometimes these things loom around in the air while we wait in fear of their arrival. While we wait in fear for that new boss or the announcement regarding layoffs, our behavior puts us at a disadvantage. Our language puts us at a disadvantage. We behave and talk as though we are the victim underdogs waiting to be slaughtered. Fear is not associated with strength, empowerment or confidence. When these unknowns are looming, constantly check yourself to make sure you are behaving and communicating in a manner consistent with strength, empowerment, and confidence. Everyone will take notice, including the decision makers. Take the unknown and make it known to others that no matter what happens you are going to succeed.

Change

By now most people know that the only constant is change, yet we behave in a manner that is contrary to this knowledge. When announcements are made at work regarding reorganizations and changes in processes or reporting relationships we immediately go into a phase of resistance and mourning. We tell anyone who will listen how disappointed we are and how the leadership team just doesn't have a clue. We bring up the old way of doing things meeting after meeting. And worse is when we try to sabotage the new way of doing things or even the new person in charge of the new processes. Again, these behaviors are driven by fear. We are afraid to leave our warm, comfortable cozy process, project or supervisor. We are afraid that we might be uncomfortable and that we will not be able to meet or exceed expectations for the latest challenge. We are afraid that our old routine is the only way we can be effective. We are afraid of being moved into a new space before even trying it out. We know the old, we like the old; so why change? The fastest way to be labeled a problem is to be fearful of change. Push back and questioning the validity of change is acceptable if your intent to protect the greater good is known and believable. However, when you are resisting for the purpose of self-preservation, you are essentially shooting yourself in the foot. You will never be viewed as a progressive leader with this attitude.

Follow these steps if you find yourself constantly resisting change:

- Be pragmatic. In other words, kick the tires before you buy the car. And if you see a real problem with the car, develop a solution so that you can drive a well-functioning car off the lot. Never resist change without a plan to resolve the issue for which the change has been designed.

- Be future focused. People who are viewed as strategic thinkers maintain a future focus. Their language, behaviors and entire orientation are focused on what is necessary to take the organization to the next level. The future is unknown and that can spark fear in some, but push through the fear. Those who focus on the past are typically viewed as being "in the weeds" with limited capabilities for making a true impact.

- Stay away from the following phrases:
    - "This is the way we have always done it." Growth, learning, development and progress require forward movement. Change has to occur in order to keep pace with the future.
    - "We tried that 2 years ago and it did not work." If you have already tried something in the past, it is okay to try it again with new leaders in place and new players around the table.

Instead, use language that builds on what can be done. When you trust the process, fear is not in the equation. So trust. Consider the following phrases:

- "Let's take advantage of this opportunity to develop ourselves as leaders."
- "Instead of remaining comfortable, let's really challenge ourselves to raise the bar."
- "Let's trust the data and focus on the goal with confidence."
- "I believe we have the capabilities to get this done."
- "Nothing stays the same. It's going to either get worse or improve. Let's push to move forward."

Personality

There are individuals who worry quite a bit. Now you may believe that worry and fear are not the same but it is a fact that worry often leads to fear. It is also important to note that those who worry send messages (intentional or unintentional) to others regarding their ability to be strong, empowered, or confident. In fact, worriers are often viewed as less capable of handling pressure. Do not allow fear to cause you to constantly worry. It WILL show.

Fear of Loss

One Day Sale! Hurry, supplies are limited! Only two rooms left! All of these phrases are used to capitalize on our natural fear of loss. When we fear we are going to lose something, our behavior changes dramatically. If you fear you are going to lose your job or lose an opportunity for promotion, you may do things that go against your character. Do not allow fear to cause you to behave in a manner that you will regret. If you lose your job or miss out on a promotion, it is imperative that you adopt the belief that something better is on the horizon. After you fully adopt this belief, go for it. Fight for it. Take action. You will land on your feet if you put the work in.

In the case of Rosa Parks, fear would have caused her to stand up on that bus. It was courage that caused her to keep her seat and change the world.

For Thought...Audrey's Courageous Stand

For the past year, Audrey and her peers had often discussed their boss' unethical behavior. When Audrey's boss issued a mandate to the team that required them to perform tasks that were not in alignment with the organization's policies and procedures, Audrey decided this was the last straw. The team reacted by spreading their disappointment and discontent all over the company. As a result of all the swirling gossip, Audrey's boss' boss called an impromptu skip level meeting where she asked Audrey and her peers about unethical behaviors that were allegedly being committed by Audrey's boss. Because of fear, Audrey was the only one who was willing to speak up in the meeting with her boss's boss and tell the truth. When it really mattered, Audrey was the only one who was courageously willing to take a stand and blow the whistle on her boss' bad behavior. Now, Audrey is facing retaliation from her boss and a loss of partnership with her peers. Audrey, who is an excellent performer, decided to resign her position. She resigned because her work values were not in alignment with the organization's values. She did not resign out of fear. Audrey moved on to a new opportunity where she is already being considered for a promotion. When Audrey reflects on that fateful day when she took a stand, she remains confident that the courage of her convictions will ultimately lead to her long term success.

Feedback

"Whoever loves discipline loves knowledge, but whoever hates correction is stupid." *Proverbs 12:1 NIV*

Sometimes failure to get ahead has a lot to do with the fact that we fail to effectively give and receive feedback. The purpose of giving or receiving feedback is to develop the individual who is receiving it. One has to receive the feedback, put all defensiveness to the side, and apply the corrections in their work world. Giving feedback can destroy careers as well if it is not delivered correctly. One way this plays out is gaining the reputation of offending or belittling others. Consider the art of feedback as prescribed in this book as you continue your career journey.

Q: What is feedback?
A: Feedback is information resulting from an observed behavior or outcome.

Feedback in the workplace should never be based on subjective opinion. It should be anchored by time and place, consist of an observable behavior and be supported by impact. Unfortunately, this is often not the case.

Q: Why do we give and receive feedback?
A: To continuously improve or develop in a specific area.

Think about the last form of feedback you gave to anyone. What was your motive? Were you trying to build that person up or tear them down? If you were making a sincere attempt to develop that person, congratulations. You completed the first step in giving effective feedback. If you were lashing out at that person, attempting to "one up" them, prove that you were right and they were wrong, or if your intent was to hurt their feelings, your intentions were not in alignment with the true spirit of feedback.

Think about the last time you received feedback. What did you learn? How did you use it? Responding to positive feedback usually involves appreciation and feelings of warmth and respect. Most people love to <u>receive</u> positive feedback. It just feels good. Responding to constructive feedback usually involves defensiveness, denial and a loss of desire to partner with that person. Increase your self-awareness of your physiological cues associated with getting upset or defensive.

Examples of physiological cues associated with defensiveness:

- Feeling heat around your face
- Eye twitching
- Increased heart rate

Examples of defensive body language:

- Clinched fists
- Eye rolling
- Sighing out loud
- Raised voice volume

The key is to be aware of when you are experiencing these physiological cues or exhibiting defensive body language. Raising your self-awareness around these symptoms and behaviors enhances your Emotional Intelligence or EQ. Emotional Intelligence (EQ) is important for success because demonstrating inappropriate emotions or deviant behaviors consistently can and will derail your career. One of the best strategies for becoming less defensive is to inhale deeply through your nose and exhale deeply through your nose. This will diminish your desire to turn on your "fight or flight" mechanism. Instead, deep breathing will give you a sense of calm and clarity. If you need to say something, say "That's interesting. Please tell me more." This implies that you are seeking to truly understand, not to strike back. Once you have calm and clarity, facilitate a discussion focused on solutions to the problem. In your facilitation of this solution-oriented dialogue, remember your techniques for staying calm and seeking clarity.

Whether feedback is positive or constructive, it should always be viewed as a tool designed to offer support or to issue a challenge for continuous improvement.

Delivering Constructive Feedback

Most people don't mind giving or receiving positive feedback. The challenge usually comes with giving and receiving constructive feedback. Giving constructive feedback is difficult for some because they are anticipating conflict. For these people, avoiding conflict is more important than delivering constructive feedback. If you have reservations about giving constructive feedback, take yourself out of the equation and focus your feedback on specific points of data, not feelings or opinions. If you are a manager holding an employee accountable for repeatedly showing up late to work, reference the attendance policy. Present the employee with a copy of the policy and facilitate a discussion about the major points of the policy and the stated consequences of not following the policy. This diminishes the thought of you vs. the employee and makes it about the employee vs. the policy. It is also helpful to plan the difficult conversation by making notes of the key points you want to address. The most critical step in delivering difficult feedback is to keep the conversation on track. When conflict does arise because the receiver is becoming defensive, the receiver will likely begin to bring up irrelevant facts. They may bring up other people, get overly emotional, or accuse you of doing something wrong. If you allow yourself to "chase the rabbit" down a path of all things irrelevant, your objectives will not get accomplished and you could potentially get yourself in a lot of emotionally fueled trouble. Call a "time out" immediately if conflict arises and walk away. The "time out" can last 5 minutes or 5 days as long as you resume the meeting within a reasonable and agreed upon period of time. Remember, the receiver may introduce irrelevant facts or get emotional to avoid having to deal with the feedback. Stay calm, stay focused, and rely on data, not your opinion or hearsay when giving constructive feedback.

The Steps for Delivering Effective Feedback

Step One:

When delivering positive or constructive feedback, it is critical that the sender and receiver are on the same page. This also prevents the receiver from playing the "I don't know what you are talking about" game or the "I don't remember" game. The best way to do this is for the sender to state the time, place, environment or deadline associated with the point of feedback.

Step Two:
Only provide feedback on things that can be observed. In other words, do not provide feedback based on feelings or opinions. Feedback must be based on facts.

Step Three:
After the observable action has been stated, the sender should then inform the receiver of the outcomes that resulted from their actions or behaviors. This portion of the feedback can be an opinion or evaluation.

Step Four:
Ask what they believe next steps should be. Now you can engage in a two-way discussion. This will require you to have a listening ear. Be open to what they have to say. Try to steer the conversation away from defensiveness and denial should that occur.

Step Five:
Determine the best time to revisit this conversation. Remember, this is a process, not a one shot deal. Do not wait too long but give the issue a moment to breathe. One week is a solid recommendation for coming back to the table to discuss solutions and set direction.

Examples of Excellent Feedback:

Step One: Communicate the Setting or Environment	Step Two: Only State Observable Actions	Step Three: Share the Outcomes/Results
• Yesterday morning while you were making copies in the copy room...	• You left a very important document with sensitive information on the copier...	• Had this information leaked to the rest of the team, it would have caused unnecessary panic and chaos.
• The day the 3rd quarter report was due...	• I discovered you had turned the report in a week ahead of schedule...	• As a result, we appeared prepared and very organized in the eyes senior leadership. Great job!
• Earlier today during our staff meeting...	• You hit the conference table with your fist...	• I felt you were angry with me. Is there anything we need to discuss?

Remember to include steps 4 & 5 to begin the process of generating resolution and positive dialogue. Feedback whether it be positive or constructive is designed to develop and support the recipient. Look in the mirror to determine if this is truly your motive when giving feedback. If you are the recipient of feedback, positive or constructive, make an effort to say "thank you" in response to the feedback. This will go a long way in building **trust** in your communication with the sender.

Finger Pointing

"'Have you eaten from the tree that I commanded you not to eat from?' The man said, 'The woman you put here with me—she gave me some fruit from the tree, and I ate it.' Then the LORD God said to the woman, 'What is this you have done?' The woman said, 'The serpent deceived me, and I ate.'" Genesis 3:11-13 NIV

Finger pointing has been in existence since the beginning of the world. As soon as God confronted Adam for eating the forbidden fruit, Adam blamed Eve. Eve in turn blamed the serpent and the rest is history. This in essence ruined Adam's lifestyle as he had to leave the Garden of Eden where he had it good and go to work. Today, we point the finger at our spouses for not replacing the toilet paper roll. We point the finger at our kids for bringing home bad grades, we point the finger at our co-workers for dropping the ball, we blame our boss for making our lives miserable, our boss points the finger at consultants when it is time to terminate their problem employee, we point the finger at the food industry for making us fat, we even blame the President of the United States for all of our financial woes. The intent in blaming others is to take the heat off of self. The only problem with this is that if you always blame other people, nothing will ever improve because 9 times out of 10, the problem is YOU! Yes, it is you.

- YOU can change the toilet paper roll yourself.
- YOU can help your kids with their homework and meet with their teachers on a regular basis.
- YOU can pick up your co-worker's slack and mentor him or her on time management tips or skill development.
- YOU can stop giving your boss so much control over your happiness.
- YOU can even manage your boss, through strategic communication, to improve the relationship between the two of you.
- YOU can make tough decisions without having to throw someone else under the bus.

- YOU can stop eating fried foods every night and hit the gym every day.
- YOU can even take control of your family's financial health by paying off your debts and saving for your financial future. The President cannot prohibit you from working whether it is on a job or in your own business.

The point is, when you get ready to point the finger and blame someone else for the issue you are experiencing, look in the mirror. You are choosing to passively blame others. You are choosing not to stand on your own two feet and make a decision to work your way out of the situation you have found yourself in.

Accepting Responsibility is a leadership competency that few people ever properly master. This is most likely because accepting responsibility may involve admitting that you were wrong or that you did not do something very well. Being vulnerable is perceived as risky by some because they fear they will be viewed as incompetent. Usually, this is not the case. Those who expose a vulnerable side actually show their humanity which builds **trust** over time. The other challenge is that taking responsibility almost always involves additional work. Most people do not like to feel vulnerable and many people shy away from hard work; consequently, they never reach the level in life they want to reach. A good coach credits the team after a win. A good coach also takes responsibility for a loss. The concept of the captain going down with the ship speaks to the captain's responsibility for everything and everyone on board.

Raise your level of self-awareness in regards to your finger pointing behavior. YOU might be pointing the finger if you are:

- Complaining about what an individual did or did not do
- Throwing someone under the bus by shifting responsibility from you to them.
- Expecting everyone else to solve the problem
- Waiting for someone else to take responsibility

Accepting responsibility, rather than blaming others is the true mark of a good leader.

Turn By Turn Directions

The Three F's: Fear, Feedback & Finger Pointing

Most people are in denial about fear, feedback and finger pointing. Elephants in the room destroy the foundation of individual morale, relationships, teams, and ultimately organizations. You have to decide what role to take to get others to acknowledge that the elephants are present and to put in the work to make sure the the elephants leave the building.

Fear

People do not own the fact that they are fearful. Instead they continue on in torment. That's right torment. Where there is fear there is torment and that is unacceptable, especially in the workplace. Many aspects of communication can breed fear. The key to combating fearful communication is to check your expectations around the timeliness and appropriateness of the communications. It may not be the right time for information to be dispensed. The content of the communication may also be inappropriate for certain groups. Always seek to understand first. Failed communication resulting in fear is often born out of misunderstanding the intent of the sender. Ask questions when you are left wondering. More importantly, ask the person(s) who actually have the answers. Otherwise you are gossiping. Finally, increase your self-awareness on how you naturally respond to the unknown, change, and the fear of loss. You can **choose** to fight against fear and be of good courage in each of these instances.

Feedback

Always give and receive feedback with the goal of development. Ask yourself, "How can I give or take information and use it to develop myself or others?" Be sure to deliver feedback in a manner that anchors the date, time, place or environment, reveals specific and factual behaviors or action, and relays the ultimate outcomes or results that will lead to next steps in terms of development. When giving or receiving constructive feedback, be aware of your physiological cues that trigger defensive or intense behavior. Know when to "take a time" out or when to hit the "pause button". Feedback is a powerful tool and should never be used as a destructive weapon.

Finger Pointing

Focus on your role in the challenge and the solution to the challenge. Do not focus on where to place the blame. Blaming others is like intentionally saying, "Hey let's all get on a Hamster wheel and run as fast as we can in the name of progress!" Blaming others is a total waste of time. Continuous improvement of self and others should substitute blame for the greater good.

Trust

The trust builder for this chapter is **responsibility acceptance**. When you accept responsibility for solving a challenge, you are not fearful, you are totally open to feedback, you are pointing the finger at yourself. More importantly, you are potentially making yourself vulnerable; you are saying "I'm not perfect but I am committed to resolving the situation." Responsibility acceptance makes you a trust worthy, courageous human which will go a long way on your quest to becoming an influential leader.

Your Road Map

Describe the most beneficial concepts you learned as a result of studying this chapter. Explain how you found these concepts applicable in your work life.

____

____

____

____

Considering a current challenge you are having, list two strategies or commitments you are willing make as a result of studying this chapter.

1. ____
2. ____

List three individuals/resources you need to now engage as a result of studying this chapter.

1. ____
2. ____
3. ____

Chapter Nine

Enjoy Success and Get Over Stress!

Take the time to celebrate success and search diligently to find the "silver lining" in the midst of high stress.

As long as you work, you are going to have successes and huge wins as well as challenges with people and processes. This is the reality of working. These outcomes are predictable. If you were not aware of this reality, you are now! The question now becomes, how do you respond to successes and challenges? Do you...

- High five your peers in celebration, laugh loudly, celebrate small and large wins, or conversely, when you don't win, do you complain, become visibly upset or spread your discontent around the work environment?
- Moan and groan for a moment and then move into generating solutions, or celebrate briefly before moving onto the next challenge?
- Immediately begin to think of solutions to the challenge or move on to the next project without taking the time to celebrate successes?

Developing awareness of how you react to success and stress is the key to getting the most out of this chapter. Whether you tend to overreact or under react, people are going to form opinions regarding your behavior, and whether it is appropriate and ultimately professional. It is up to you to discover what you do really well and what you need to work on.

Enjoy Your Success

Ahhhh, the smell of sweet success. You have worked hard and it has paid off. It's time to **celebrate.** It is very important that successes are celebrated so take the time to do so and enjoy the following benefits:

10 Benefits Associated with Celebrating Successes

- Increases morale
- Fosters teambuilding
- Encourages effective communication
- Promotes positive thinking
- Builds employee loyalty
- Facilitates a culture of fun
- Inspires commitment versus compliance
- Maintains sufficient energy levels
- Shows appreciation
- Demonstrates the value the organization places on its people

A celebration does not have to mean balloons, streamers and cake in the break room with a large gathering. A celebration can be as simple as having dessert with your lunch, getting a manicure and/or pedicure, or leaving work a little early to go spend some "me time." Be creative and have fun with it. It is also important to share your success with family and friends. We often share our work-related challenges with those we love. This can cause your loved ones to have negative feelings towards your workplace. Celebrate your successes with those who mean the most, and you will foster a positive perception of your job and your organization to your loved ones.

Pre-plan your celebrations. When you embark upon a new project or set a new goal, decide what success will look like before you launch the project or set out to accomplish the goal. Then decide how you will celebrate once success is achieved. The reality is you may be the only one who gives you a celebratory pat on the back, but you must celebrate both small and large successes. Motivation is more meaningful when it comes from within.

There is **a dark side to celebrating your success**. There are people who will elevate themselves every chance they get. They are so self absorbed that their behavior is downright obnoxious. For most of these people, we have to assume positive intent. In other words, they do not mean any harm. There are, of course, those who endeavor to exalt themselves above all others by showcasing themselves and tooting their own horn until everyone around them is nauseous. The biggest problem with this is that when you consistently exalt yourself you are most likely putting others down or excluding them. **Do not become this person**. If you are this person, change your behavior today. You are choosing to promote yourself over others; in the process, you will alienate people who could have critical influence over your career path. Your celebrations should not only reflect your success, but the success of others. There is a clear difference between celebrating and boasting or bragging. Plan celebrations that are inclusive of everyone who made it happen, no matter how big or small their role. It's always a great idea to thank others for their help and their support. A hand written thank you note goes a long way in this world of high tech communication. When times are tough and challenges are difficult, those you celebrated with and thanked in the past will show up to support you.

Get Over Stress!

Life is not fair. Stress happens. Many of us have been there, done that and own the t-shirt when it comes to these two sayings. Here's the deal: if you work you will have stress and you will be disappointed with many aspects of your work life.

Stress

The following five strategies will help you to tackle stress and get over it more quickly so you can move on to bigger and better things.

1. **Daily Activity** – The strategy of daily activity simply means move your body and increase your normal activity level. This is not the same as a daily hour long high intensity aerobic workout. (Of course if you are already putting in that level of exercise, please continue!) This may mean getting off of the subway a stop early and walking the extra blocks, taking the stairs, parking as far away from the door as possible, doing push-ups during commercials, lifting 5-8 pound weights while talking on the phone, or simply taking a walk during lunch or after dinner. The key is to move more and to do it every single day. Why every day you ask? Because you deal with stress every day!

2. **Deep breathing** – Seriously! When we are stressed our body naturally wants to fight back or run away. Breathing in deeply through your nose and exhaling deeply through your nose continuously for a few minutes tells your brain that everything is going to be okay.

3. **Focus on the things you can control, release the things you cannot control** – For most people low control equals high stress. **Reality Check:** There are some things you will never be able to control. Direct your energy towards things you can control. This should leave little room for those things you cannot control. Make peace with those things you cannot control. If the things you have low control over start to stress you out, redirect your thoughts and choose to be at peace with those processes, decisions and ultimately results that you cannot control. At some point, you are going to have to **trust** that the things you have low control over are going to work out and ultimately benefit the greater good.

There may be times when your stress is related to the sheer volume of everything you have to do in your life. Heavy volume at work, a hectic travel schedule, the demands of marriage and children, maintaining your home and cars, bills, your weight, your overall health... Need I go on? Again take control and only focus on the things you can truly control in short doses. Pull out your smart phone or tablet and set the timer for 20 minutes. Work on one of your stressors for 20 minutes and when that timer goes off, take a break! Literally walk away. When you are ready, set the timer again and do something different. Another strategy for overcoming the feeling of being overwhelmed is to get organized. Make a list, develop a schedule, put things where they belong. Spend 20 minutes getting organized every day.

4. **Get over it** – Once you have experienced a setback, a negative interaction with someone else, bad news, or have been generally mistreated, you have a choice to make. You can stew in the hurt and sadness or vow to get revenge. You can even be angry and hold a grudge against someone else for years to come. Please realize that when you do this, you are giving someone or something else power over you. You are literally handing them power over you on a silver platter. You may even be on the road to derailing your career. You have to find a way to get over it as quickly as you can. The funny thing is that in situations such as this, half of those involved have already gotten over it, and are wondering why there is still so much tension and attitude. The other half of those involved in the challenge will harbor the situation forever and earn the image of an angry, uncooperative, unprofessional team member.

   The first step to getting over it is to realize that you are in the mode of hurt, sadness, doom and gloom. Once you have that awareness, you have to be willing to take steps to claw your way out of that mindset. One strategy for doing this is to **laugh**. Watch your favorite comedy, call an old friend and reminisce about the hilarious time you did something crazy, go to YouTube and watch funny videos, laugh. Laughter really is the best medicine.

   Now that you have laughed so hard your cheeks hurt, you can now direct your energies towards gaining a **future focus**. Think about how your role and your relationships at work will look 6 months to one year out if you do not change your attitude. You are in a fishbowl and people are watching you even if you think they are not. Even in the midst of stressful situations, your attitude, thoughts and behaviors must reflect the leader you want to be.

5. Set the **Ultimate Goal** and focus on it – Where do you ultimately want to go in your career? Is your goal to achieve a Vice President position? Do you want to work in the same position you are in until you retire? Do you eventually want to own your own business? Do you want to retire early? Decide what your ultimate goal is and make it your focal point in times of trouble. When stressors hit immediately ask yourself this question, "How will my behavior over the next few minutes, hours, days, weeks and months related to this situation get me closer to my ultimate goal?" Beginning with the end in mind is **Strategic Thinking**. More often than not, you will be successful if you think through situations and form an intentional approach or strategy that is designed to support your ultimate goal. Don't be the reason you are unable to succeed. Allow your ultimate goal to be a guiding light in darkness, a rudder when you are directionless, and a compass when you are lost. Set your ultimate goal today and allow it to get you through the stressful times in your career.

Disappointment

Disappointment causes stress. We become disappointed when our expectations are not met. Think about a time when you were disappointed in a relationship with another person. Maybe you expected your husband to repair things around the house when you married him. Now 2 years into the marriage you see that he is not handy nor does he have any interest in maintaining your home. You are disappointed. You may even be angry. **Reality Check:** Your expectations were out of whack, especially if the topic of home repairs did not come up in discussion before you said "I do". If you are not careful, your disappointment is going to damage the marriage. You have a few options:

- Get angry and start fight, after fight, after fight, and **lose focus** on the ultimate goal of "till death do you part".
- Learn how to repair and maintain the home on your own, be happy with your newly developed skills, and focus on the ultimate goal of "till death do you part".
- Hire a handyman, be happy and focus on the ultimate goal of "till death do you part".

The same principles apply at work. If you are disappointed because your expectations for how your boss should reward and recognize your accomplishments differs from how he or she actually rewards and recognizes your accomplishments, do not start telling yourself that your boss does not appreciate you. If you tell yourself this story, chances are you are not going to be a loyal employee who is 110% committed to supporting your boss and giving your best to the organization. You have a few options:

- **Lose focus**, be compliant, and at times deviant, going through the motions of satisfactory performance while looking for another job, all the while spreading your discontent about how your boss either does not value others or plays favorites.
- Propose a rewards and recognition system for your department with clear, objective criteria for receiving rewards and recognition.
- Reward and recognize your boss for his or her accomplishments. Demonstrate the leadership behaviors for your boss that you would like to see reflected in the leadership of your team.

Success and stress are two things that we know are going to happen in life. Stress is not always a bad thing and success to some means failure to others. Use stress to motivate you and inspire you to do greater things. Enjoy your success by thanking and lifting up as many people as you can. Support your stress through trust of others concerning the things you cannot control and strategically thinking of ways to achieve your ultimate goals. Stay focused on the goal and don't let stress deter you from success.

Turn By Turn Directions

Stress Management Self Check

Now that you have read this chapter, rate yourself. How would you rate yourself on a scale of one to ten, ten being indicative of your excellent ability to handle stress and success?

Success __________

1 – Poor 5 – Average 10 - Excellent

Stress __________

1 – Poor 5 – Average 10 – Excellent

If you scored yourself a 5 or less, this is your opportunity to identify specific challenges, and develop goals and action plans designed to support your development. Take the time to do this and hold yourself accountable. Your career depends on it.

If you scored yourself a 5 or more, validate your scores by asking the person who knows you best how they would rate you. If this person agrees with your rating within 2 points, this is great news! You have good awareness around this concept. Now your job is to protect the positive perceptions of your behavior during successes and stressors moving forward. If this person disagrees with your rating by more than 2 points, ask and be open to their feedback. This means listen to understand, not to respond or defend. This is a clear opportunity to identify specific challenges, and develop goals and action plans designed to support your development.

Celebrating Success

The best things about celebrating your successes are the benefits that go along with the celebrations. All of the benefits described earlier in the chapter contribute to a better YOU and a greater good. Building a culture of celebration breeds a culture of valuing and appreciating others as well as a culture that can take a punch and still thrive. As a caution, remember to celebrate in support of each other, not in an attempt to exalt yourself. You will become the person everyone loves to despise if you push other people down while promoting yourself.

Getting Over Stress

The five steps to getting over stress are all things that are easy to implement. The challenge will be in your willingness to commit to these five steps. Are you truly willing to engage in daily activity? You will have days where you are too busy, too tired or too disinterested. It will be up to you to decide and do it. The same concept applies to deep breathing, which you may find silly. If these five strategies do not resonate with you, be creative and come up with other strategies. The point is, if you choose not to create a strategic approach to dealing with stress, understand that you are choosing to be stressed. It's your choice to make.

When you are dealing with conflict and stress, ask yourself, "where do I ultimately want to land when my life or career is said and done?" Allow the answer to that question to guide your decisions and behavior in the midst of conflict and stress. This may require that you hold your tongue, or conversely, it may require that you speak your mind. Maybe you will have to reset your expectations and take action. Beginning with the end in mind is **Strategic Thinking.** This type of thinking will get you through to your ultimate life goals.

Trust

By now it should be clear that trust is critical for success. Trust of others is an effective strategy for dealing with stress. When you experience a situation where you have little to no control and your stress levels are steadily increasing it should be a clear indicator for you to let your issues go and trust those whose job it is to make decisions or carry out the plan. If you choose not to trust the people in charge or the process in place, you are setting yourself up to be stressed. In turn, your behavior could come across to others as unsupportive, unprofessional, resistant, or negative. These behaviors could haunt you for the rest of your career if those with influence interpret your behavior as being inconsistent with taking a leadership role or taking on more responsibility. These behaviors could even lead to you being demoted or terminated. Well placed trust is a strategic maneuver with significant implications. Still, it's a choice. The question is will you make the right choice for your career? The first step in the right direction is having self awareness around the fact that your stress is a direct result of you not trusting the leaders and/or the decisions that are being made. When you recognize where your stress is coming from, consider the worst case scenario associated with you fully trusting, not necessarily agreeing with, the leader and their decisions. If the worst case scenario does not involve death, injury or imprisonment, let it go and trust the process. Your ability to truly trust will significantly decrease your stress and increase the trust and credibility that others assign to you.

Your Road Map

Plan your next celebration in anticipation of an upcoming success. Be creative!

____

____

____

____

List your greatest stressors and describe the strategies that best support your management of those stressors.

1. ____
2. ____
3. ____

List three opportunities that you have had, but did not take advantage of, to trust a person or a process. What will you do differently now that you have studied this chapter?

1. ____
   ____
2. ____
   ____
3. ____
   ____

Chapter Ten

Navigating Different Approaches to Managing Change

When managing change, depersonalize the change process. It is easy to reject a person. It is much more difficult to reject facts supported by data. Allow the facts to speak while you, the person, remain silent.

There really is no such thing as "resistance to change". Some people are ignorant of what the change entails. Consequently, they resist the unknown, not the change itself. Ignorance also provokes fear of making mistakes. Since no one knows everything, we are all at risk of making mistakes and we may all "resist" change from time to time. In reality we are resisting the likelihood of making mistakes. Then there are those that are comfortable in their current state. Again, they may not necessarily be resistant to change. Instead, it may just be a matter of them learning why they should actually be uncomfortable with their current state. This will energize these individuals to seek comfort in a different set of circumstances. The lesson this chapter will leave you with is simply that what people often perceive as resistance to change is an approach to change different from their own.

Change Readiness Self Check: Find yourself under the following list of behaviors.

- ☐ Meets change with optimism and a spirit of experimentation
- ☐ Is open to change, as long as the change has been deemed necessary
- ☐ Meets change with hesitation, resistance, fear or even pessimism rather than optimism

Certainly we have all come to terms with the fact that change is constant. However, everyone approaches change differently. Do not misinterpret diverse approaches to change as resistance to change or even embracing change. Change is presented to us in many different forms. Sometimes we are forced to navigate through the changing landscape of the industry we work within. Other times we are expected to learn something new very quickly. Innovation also offers us the catalyst to change in that we are often expected to come up with new and competitive solutions. This chapter will focus on change as it is met by the three behavioral descriptions listed above in the **Self Check**. Remember to hold up the proverbial mirror as you assess the way you approach and navigate change.

Meets Change with Optimism and a Spirit of Experimentation
At a macro level, every industry in every market has to embrace this change philosophy in order to grow and ultimately thrive. At a micro level, individuals who subscribe to this philosophy may be viewed as innovative, creative, eccentric, unrealistic, or just plain annoying. The reality is, these individuals are needed and are quite frankly in demand. However, those who are eager to change desperately need to engage openly with those that are slower to change as well as those who are resistant to change, in order to create balanced, practical innovative change.

If you are this person: Congratulations! This is a strength that you should market to organizations and key business leaders. Continue to be bold in terms of having confidence in the solutions and creative approaches you propose. However, be open to the wisdom and advice of those that want to slow the pace or all out preserve the current state. Their wisdom could save you the time and money associated with re-work. Their wisdom could also save your reputation.

Point of Focus: Your focus should be the machine we call The System. Think SWOT, Strengths and Weaknesses of inside of the organization as well as Opportunities and Threats coming from outside of the organization. Your innovative approach to process and readiness for change of the current state will provide the competitive advantage your organization is looking for. Lead with confidence in this area and you will be successful.

If you are working with this person and you do not share this philosophy on change: Be thankful that this person is on your team. They most likely hold the key to the team's next great success story. In reality, I know you find this person mildly to extremely annoying but you must get over that ASAP! It is your job to leverage your knowledge, skills, and abilities with their innovative, crazy ideas to make a little bit of magic. Do not tell them what to do and talk at them. Innovative, change-ready, creative types do not respond to that communication style. Instead, ask them lots of critical thinking, thought provoking questions. In other words, you want to lead them to the point of considering your perspective. You do not want to drag them there kicking and screaming. Finally, do not forget that you are grateful for them so **trust their ideas** and help them get off the ground. If your process for managing change gets rocky, embrace it! This means diverse views are in the mix which will surely yield progress. You are the anchor that ensures stable success over time. They are the helium that floats the next big thing. Together, success will be yours for many years to come.

Is Open to Change, as Long as the Change has Been Deemed Necessary
The role of those that fall into this category is to support the successful execution and sustainability of the change taking place. Individuals who subscribe to this philosophy may be viewed as data driven, inquisitive, delaying progress, or cautious supporters of change. In some cases, they may be viewed as resistors of change. The reality is, if these individuals did not exist, the failure/disaster rate of changes implemented would more than quadruple.

If you are this person: Congratulations! You are the great equalizer. You love change, as long as it has been qualified, vetted and deemed necessary. You do your homework and you are passionate about protecting your interest and the interest of the organization you serve. They key to your success lies in the way you communicate your approach to change because your approach can be easily misinterpreted for resistance. Be sure to convey that you are all for the change and that you are all for protecting the greater good. Make sure that the vetting and research you require is visible to others because in the absence of information, people may decide that you are behaving in a manner that is resistant to the proposed change.

Point of Focus: It will be very important that you monitor yourself to be sure that you are not taking your investigative approach too far. Stay as neutral as possible so that your decision benefits the ultimate impact on the organization. Your role is to be sure the team is making data driven decisions that will support the execution of the change over time. Your role is not to collect so much data that you cause the process to lose momentum and the team to lose morale. It is also important for these individuals to include those eager for change and those resistant to change in their data collection. By taking both sides into account, you can create a more accurate context for the other data points you are considering. This also presents a great opportunity to bridge any differences that may exist on the team.

If you are working with this person and you do not share this philosophy on change: Be thankful that this person is on your team. By gathering and presenting valuable data that will support organizational impact, these individuals will either save you from making a HUGE mistake in moving forward with the proposed change or they will encourage you to step out of your comfort zone and embrace the change movement. Chances are these individuals will present an argument that you do not agree with. This is where <u>**trust**</u> and openness come into play. Objectively consider the data and put the organization, not your agenda, first. This will allow you to leverage the talents and diversity effectively resulting in big wins for the team.

Meets Change with Hesitation, Fear or Even Pessimism Rather than Optimism

The old saying, "If it ain't broke, don't fix it" truly has some merit.

If you are this person: It is critical that you are aware of and accept the fact that people label you as a resistor of change. Your focus must be on serving the greater good, not on putting up road blocks to progress. Do not be afraid to fight for what you think is right. However, because you tend to go against the grain of change, create a strategic response for every challenge you present to others. Ensure your challenge statement includes the overall outcomes and how the overall outcomes will positively and significantly serve the greater good. Also, be strategic and pick your battles. There is nothing worse than being labeled something with a historically negative connotation. Surprise your teammates from time to time. You might just enjoy going with the flow.

Point of Focus: Examine yourself when you are in the mode of preserving your current state to determine what it is you really want. Once you have determined what you really want, allow everything else to progress. Communicate you motive and present an argument that serves the greater good, NOT your own biased beliefs. If you serve the team, the team will serve you.

If you are working with this person and you do not share this philosophy on change: Be thankful that this person is on your team. Again, do not refer to them as being resistant to change. These individuals could save you from making a HUGE mistake in moving forward with the proposed change. Chances are these individuals will present an argument that you do not agree with. This is an opportunity to give and receive feedback. Acknowledge any insights you gain from this person and show appreciation for their diverse perspective. This person represents stability which supports sustainability. The reality is that change is inevitable; however, change does not have to occur 100 miles per hour. This is where **trust** and openness come into play. Remember change begins with ownership. Objectively consider all of the data and put the organization, not your agenda, first. Then work with this person to see what parts of the change process they are willing to own. This may require that you co-create new aspects of the change process for this person to own. People rarely reject something that they own. This will allow you to leverage everyone's talents as well as presenting diversity. This approach will effectively result in big wins for the team.

We often do not want to change because we don't trust what will come as a result. At times we do not trust those who do not want to change because we question whether or not they have our best interest at heart. Trust goes both ways. Just understand that if you decide not to give trust, you will not receive it and you may diminish your chances for true success.

Turn By Turn Directions

Don't be so quick to call "resistance to change."

Appreciating the diversity of people's approaches to change can propel not only your career, but the overall effectiveness of an organization. Teams and organizations need people who are ready to jump right into change. However, teams and organizations also need people who want to validate the need for change as well as those who do not see the need for change at all. Every approach to change has a role in supporting the overall effectiveness of the organization. The magic happens when the team or the team's leader is able to leverage this diversity to formulate a well thought out plan of execution with contingencies. When everyone's perspective is valued and appreciated, everyone will buy in to the overall goal.

Self-check for greater self awareness.

Once you find yourself in the following list of behaviors, start to think about how you might use your approach to support the people and processes around you. Support is the key word here. Some of you may need to pull back at times and others of you may need to push yourself out of your comfort zone. The key is for you to have greater self-awareness of your approach to change and the impact you are having on your team.

- Meets change with optimism and a spirit of experimentation
- Is open to change, as long as the change has been deemed necessary
- Meets change with hesitation, resistance, fear or even pessimism rather than optimism

Devise strategies for yourself as well as your strategies for working with others.

Now that you know something new and concrete about yourself, develop a few strategies to put your new awareness into action. The results associated with implementing these new strategies will not only impress you but they can potentially change the quality of your career. In formulating strategies for those who do not share your approach see it as a grand opportunity to finally do something constructive about a long-running challenge or new challenges that emerge. You can choose to have strife and conflict with others OR you can choose to create a partnership by leveraging diversity.

Trust

Change and trust go hand in hand. Withholding trust will not move things forward. At times we think others are resistant to change when really they do not trust those who want the change. Other times we withhold trust for those who change readily because we question their knowledge and experience. In reality, withholding trust can create perceptions that you are resistant to change. In addition, it may create a feeling that you do not have a high regard for the change-ready person's knowledge, skills and abilities. The bottom line is that when change is concerned trust will come into play. Incorporate giving and receiving trust in your change strategies for optimal results.

Your Road Map

According to the Self Check in this chapter, what is your approach to change and what do you see as your greatest challenge pertaining to your change approach?

____

____

____

____

List 3 strategies you can implement pertaining to your planned approach to change.

1. ______________________________________
2. ______________________________________
3. ______________________________________

List 3 strategies you can implement in terms of dealing with those who approach change differently than you do (two strategies for each differing change approach).

1. ______________________________________
2. ______________________________________
3. ______________________________________
4. ______________________________________

Chapter Eleven

Your Destination is Ahead on the Right. Use Caution If You Start to Think you Have Arrived

There is never any room for arrogance or complacency. Work smart. Be humble.

You can never, ever end your quest for knowledge, learning or self improvement. Do not confuse success with "arrival". Success should be treated as an opportunity to evaluate your attitude, your work ethic, and your desire to give to others. Ironically, failure is also a good time to assess your attitude, work ethic, and desire to give to others. These three attributes applied in the right denominations will support every competency and strategy for success outlined in this book.

Attitude

The old saying, "Your attitude determines your altitude", is essentially saying a healthy and positive attitude will take you to the highest heights in your career. Conversely, an unhealthy and poor attitude will lead to certain career derailment. It is very difficult to have a positive attitude when overtime pay has just been cut, positions are being eliminated, and your boss is the most evil person to ever walk the face of the earth. The key to maintaining a positive attitude is self awareness. As you know by now, self awareness is one of the major keys to being successful at work. In particular, you must be aware of how your negativity impacts others. Approaching challenges, change, and difficult people with a positive attitude is the number one strategy for overcoming and resolving significant issues. Seek to understand what you can learn and what the silver lining in your cloud actually is. After launching a positive approach to your challenge, you have to monitor yourself on a daily basis. As the challenge evolves, so will your attitude. Be sure to keep your attitude in check throughout. Remember, the best way to establish and maintain a positive attitude in the midst of trying times is to decide what piece of the challenge you can truly commit to and stay positive around that piece. Eventually, your commitment to be positive will expand to other things.

Work Ethic

A slacker is defined as anyone who does not use his or her time wisely to get their work done, or who causes slowdowns or disruptions in the work environment thereby increasing or intensifying the work load for others. Slackers are very irritating to high performers. Having a good work ethic is not only great for team morale and organizational effectiveness, but it illustrates your character and your commitment to job and ultimately your career. The greatest benefit of having a strong work ethic is that others find you extremely credible. Once you have credibility with others, your ability to build trust and gain influence with others is tremendously magnified.

Are YOU a slacker? Reflect on the following statements to determine the likelihood that others view you as a slacker. Circle the answer that best fits you. Remember, honesty is critical for self-development.

	Always	**Sometimes**	**Never**
1. How often do you volunteer to take on projects?	3	2	1
2. Would others say a typical day for you can be described as productive?	3	2	1
3. Do you typically finish work assignments ahead of schedule?	3	2	1
4. How often do you assess the quality of your work?	3	2	1
5. How often have you received feedback that you are effectively getting the job done?	3	2	1
Total Score: (Add your ratings together.)			

Scoring:

5 - 10 **Slacker!** The perception others have of you is very likely that you have a weak work ethic. What may be worse is that your credibility with others is most likely very low. This will ultimately impact your ability to influence others and to build genuine, trusting relationships. Share this assessment with someone you know very well and trust. Ask them to give you feedback on what your strengths and opportunities are for each survey item. The key for you is to fundamentally change the way you think about work. Once you change your thinking, your behavior will follow.

8 - 11 **Decent Work Ethic.** The perception others have of you is very likely that you have a good work ethic. Essentially, you fly under the radar. No one thinks of you as a slacker but you are also not the first person people think of when they need a guaranteed home run. Look at improving your work ethic as a choice. You have to choose to behave differently. Take a second look at each survey item and decide which two items you need to work on the most.

Evaluate yourself again in three months to determine whether or not your behavior has truly changed.

12 - 15 **Excellence!** is how most people describe the delivery and quality of your work. You are also viewed as being dependable and reliable. In order to take things to the next level, you want to ensure that people also perceive you as being a strategic visionary, not just a work executer. Your focus must extend beyond what is expected and the corresponding deadline. Focus on the problem you are trying to solve, what else is possible, and what the final product should be.

Desire to Give to Others

There are some people who spend their days thinking of new ways to give to others. These people are typically very happy and very blessed. In fact, if you try to give to them they will usually tell you they have everything they could ever want or need. In fact, most people who have the ability to influence and who are very successful are also very generous. Giving to others requires sacrifice. This is why most people are not generous with their time, money, and other resources. Unfortunately, some people never learn the following concept: when you give, you receive so much more than you gave. This is a fact.

If you do not have a desire to give to others, ask yourself why. Are you concerned with what you will be giving up? Do you struggle with seeing others enjoy benefits? Do you hesitate to share information in fear that you will somehow be demoted? Typically, individuals who do not freely give have some form of fear of loss. Let me assure you that this fear of loss is self imposed and completely unfounded. When you give to others, you promote yourself.

Challenge: for the next 30 days give or donate to others at least once per day. This can mean giving items or objects, money, compliments, appreciation, information, time or anything else that is on your heart to give. Make sure you are giving from the heart. Really think about what you are giving and who will be receiving your gift. My prediction is that at the end of 30 days you will be a better person while enjoying the tremendous return on your generous investment of giving.

Conclusion

Be diligent in your work, build trust and credibility with others, seek to find the opportunities in the midst of your storms, and give generously to others. The objective of this book is to put a tool in the hands of any and everyone who wants to improve the quality of their work lives. As you study the information in this book, consider how applying this information will help you at work and at home with your family and in your community. The best way to synthesize all of this information is to create and study the **Road Maps** at the end of each chapter in this book. Incorporate the **Turn by Turn Directions** at the end of each chapter of this book into your customized **Road Map**. Use this summary as your guide:

Summary of Turn By Turn Directions by Chapter

Chapter One: Perfecting Your People Skills • People Skills • Humbling Yourself • Influencing Others • Mutual Respect • Service	**Chapter Two: WorkPlace Bullying** • Use caution when labeling a bully • People who are Just Plain Mean • The Challengers • The Abuser of Power
Chapter Three: Creating Career Building Relationships • Best Friends at Work • Strategic Alliances • Workplace Adversaries	**Chapter Four: Developing True Self-Awareness** • Self Awareness • Personal Aptitude • Social Aptitude • Self/Multi-Rater Assessments
Chapter Five: Achieving Emotional Synergy with Self and Others • Achieving Work Life Synergy & Resiliency • Transforming Unmet Expectations (Disappointments) into Opportunities • Action Oriented Strategic Thinking • Just Get Over It!	**Chapter Six: New Employee Orientation** • Choosing to Work • Excellent Performers • Satisfactory Performers • Poor Performers
Chapter Seven: Organizational Culture • Work Values: Gaps vs. Alignment • Leadership Influence • Sales • Support	**Chapter Eight: Tackling the Elephants in the Room: The Truth About Why you are Not Getting Ahead** • Fear • Feedback • Finger Pointing
Chapter Nine: Enjoy Success and Get Over Stress • Stress Management Self Check • Celebrating Success • Getting Over Stress	**Chapter Ten: Navigating Different Approaches to Managing Change** • Don't be so quick to "call" resistance to change • Conduct your readiness for change self check for greater self awareness • Devise change strategies for self and others

Each set of Turn by Turn Directions also featured a Trust Theme. Trust was a consistent theme from chapter to chapter. Use the following summary as a quick reference guide for creating your Road Maps as well.

Trust Themes by Chapter

Chapter One: *When you humble yourself, you encourage others to put their trust in you.*

Chapter Two: *Trust yourself to handle difficult situations. You CAN do it!*

Chapter Three: *Within a healthy relationship, trust must be given and received by both parties.*

Chapter Four: *If you truly want to develop yourself, you must be willing to engage in and trust the feedback you are receiving, even if the feedback is NOT what you want to hear.*

Chapter Five: *If you truly want to experience resilience, learn to trust that your current state of life, work and family is all going to work together for good.*

Chapter Six: *The quality of our performance plays a major factor in how much trust others are willing to put in us.*

Chapter Seven: *Offering support for others breeds trust.*

Chapter Eight: *Consistently practicing responsibility acceptance makes you trust worthy because are consistently demonstrating vulnerability, openness to feedback, and true commitment.*

Chapter Nine: *Low control = high stress. Just let it go! In the process of letting it go, you have to trust those who have control that they will make the right decisions, even if you do agree with those decisions. Trust and let go!*

Chapter Ten: *If you choose to withhold trust from others, please understand that you are contributing to the perception that you are resistant to change.*

Trust is the golden key to your success. Use it thoughtfully and strategically to propel your career. It is important to set your sights on enjoying tremendous success throughout your career. Many of those successes will give you the illusion that you have arrived at your final destination. Big mistake! Achieving successes in your career should always serve as your indicator to ramp up your continuous improvement efforts. It is now time for you to win, and win you shall. Understand that you must approach winning as if it is only for a season. Always, always be ready to prepare for your next professional challenge to begin.

Acknowledgements

A huge thank you goes out to my editors James W. Swindell, Sr., Esquire and Jessica Carmago, English Professor at The University of North Carolina at Charlotte. Your time and attention will forever be sincerely appreciated.